Praise for *Soup*

"It's often said you get out what you put in. Same goes for how we lead our teams (at work, home, or school). In *Soup*, Jon Gordon has done a masterful job of illustrating the necessity of this point for anyone who wishes to increase their influence, build a better team, or expand their leadership effectiveness. The one who stirs the pot is the one who impacts the flavor of the soup, just as the one who leads the team is the one who creates the culture around it. This book will help you add flavor to your life, the lives of others, and your team."

—Carl Liebert
CEO, 24 Hour Fitness

"Once again, Jon cooks up a world-class recipe for business, emphasizing that the key to ultimate leadership success is enabling your employees to deliver excellence."

—Ryan Magnon
VP of Quality, The West Paces Hotel Group

"If you are ready to stir the pot and lead your team with more optimism, passion, and trust, you will love this book."

—Deborah Gilmore
President, Women's Council of REALTORS®

SOUP

A Recipe to Create a
Culture of Greatness

JON GORDON

WILEY

Copyright © 2010 by Jon Gordon. All rights reserved.

Published by John Wiley & Sons, Inc., Hoboken, New Jersey.

Published simultaneously in Canada.

Author note: This is a fictional story with fictional characters and entities (Grandma's Soup House and Soup, Inc.). It is not in any way endorsed by or associated with any real soup or food company.

No part of this publication may be reproduced, stored in a retrieval system, or transmitted in any form or by any means, electronic, mechanical, photocopying, recording, scanning, or otherwise, except as permitted under Section 107 or 108 of the 1976 United States Copyright Act, without either the prior written permission of the Publisher, or authorization through payment of the appropriate per-copy fee to the Copyright Clearance Center, Inc., 222 Rosewood Drive, Danvers, MA 01923, (978) 750-8400, fax (978) 646-8600, or on the web at www.copyright.com. Requests to the Publisher for permission should be addressed to the Permissions Department, John Wiley & Sons, Inc., 111 River Street, Hoboken, NJ 07030, (201) 748-6011, fax (201) 748-6008, or online at http://www.wiley.com/go/permissions.

Limit of Liability/Disclaimer of Warranty: While the publisher and author have used their best efforts in preparing this book, they make no representations or warranties with respect to the accuracy or completeness of the contents of this book and specifically disclaim any implied warranties of merchantability or fitness for a particular purpose. No warranty may be created or extended by sales representatives or written sales materials. The advice and strategies contained herein may not be suitable for your situation. You should consult with a professional where appropriate. Neither the publisher nor author shall be liable for any loss of profit or any other commercial damages, including but not limited to special, incidental, consequential, or other damages.

For general information on our other products and services or for technical support, please contact our Customer Care Department within the United States at (800) 762-2974, outside the United States at (317) 572-3993 or fax (317) 572-4002.

Wiley also publishes its books in a variety of electronic formats. Some content that appears in print may not be available in electronic books. For more information about Wiley products, visit our web site at www.wiley.com.

ISBN: 978-0470-48784-6

Printed in the United States of America

SKY10030042_092321

For my grandparents, Martin and Janice Gordon.
Your love made the difference.

Jon as a young boy with his grandparents
and a big pot of SOUP.

Contents

	Acknowledgments	ix
	Introduction	x
1	**Hungry**	1
2	**Grandma's Soup House**	5
3	**Grandma**	9
4	**Nancy**	13
5	**Another Bowl**	15
6	**Who Stirs the Pot Matters**	19
7	**Teachers Are Everywhere**	23
8	**Soup = Culture**	27
9	**A Culture of Greatness**	31
10	**Nightmare**	35
11	**Lead With Optimism**	39
12	**Leadership Is a Transfer of Belief**	43
13	**Guard Against Pessimism**	47
14	**The Mirror Test**	51
15	**Nancy Stirs the Pot**	53
16	**Hire Possibility Thinkers**	55
17	**A Unifying Vision**	57

18	Spread the Vision	61
19	Build Trust	63
20	Busy	67
21	The Survey	69
22	Enhance Communication	71
23	Fill the Void	75
24	Add a Big Dose of Transparency and Authenticity	79
25	Treat Them Like Family	81
26	Love	83
27	Rumors	85
28	A New Measuring Stick	89
29	Relationships	93
30	Soup Is Meant to Be Enjoyed Together	95
31	Rules Without Relationship Lead to Rebellion	97
32	The Enemies Are Busyness and Stress	99
33	Engaged Relationships	103
34	Encourage, Inspire, Empower, and Coach	105
35	A Team of Pot Stirrers	109
36	The Offer	113
37	Another Shot	117
38	40 Days of Engagement	119
39	No One Eats Alone	121
40	Success Fridays	123

41	Fill Up with Appreciation	125
42	The Ultimate Recognition Program	129
43	Great Service	131
44	Leading by Example	133
45	Friday Night	135
46	Passion	137
47	Hot Soup	141
48	Tastier Soup	143
49	The Decision	147
50	An Offer They Couldn't Refuse	149
51	The Power of Relationships	153
52	Unity	155
53	The Recipe Book	158
	Create a Culture of Greatness	*162*
	Other Books by Jon Gordon	*163*

Acknowledgments

I'm thankful for all the people who helped me stir the pot and prepare this *Soup*.

Thank you to my wife Kathryn for your continued encouragement, love, and support, and for creating a culture of greatness at home.

Thank you to my publisher, Matt Holt, and editor, Shannon Vargo, and to Beth Zipko, Kim Dayman, Larry Olson, and the rest of the team at Wiley for being more than just a publisher. You are family.

Thank you to my agent and marketing genius Daniel Decker for all your hard work, talent, and support. We are a great team.

Thank you to all the soup makers out there who stir the pot with love. I hope you enjoy this book.

Most of all, I thank God for the most important relationship in my life. Thank you for your daily bread. You nourish me and give me strength. I am here to know you, love you, and serve you.

Introduction

When I think of soup, I think of my grandmother. She loved to cook, and food and love were one and the same to her. When she cooked, she wasn't just making a meal. She was pouring out the love in her heart and sharing this love with her family. When we ate her food, we loved her back. And no soup, no matter who made it, ever tasted as good as hers. Her love made the difference.

I've discovered that who stirs the pot has an impact on what's in the pot. For example, did you know that some wine experts can determine the personality of a winemaker simply by tasting the wine? There is a common challenge experienced by chefs I call the "stirring-the-pot phenomenon." No matter how carefully different chefs follow the same recipe, the final product always varies a little bit because we can't separate who stirs the pot from what's in the pot.

The same is true in business and in every aspect of life. Every day you are stirring the pot of life, and the most important ingredient you can put into your soup is you. Your love, optimism, trust, vision, communication, authenticity, appreciation, and passion make life delicious, and the relationships you create at work and at home determine the substance and quality of your soup.

In my work with countless businesses, professional sports teams, hospitals, and school districts, I've seen firsthand how one person who grabs the spoon and decides to stir the pot can make a difference. One person who decides to bring out the best in others by sharing the best within him- or herself can transform teams and organizations.

My hope is that in reading this book, you will decide to be that person—that by your example, you will lead your company, your team, your family, your classroom, your church, your hospital. That you will invest in others and create engaged relationships that foster teamwork and create a culture of greatness.

Soup is meant to be enjoyed together. So, let us read together, learn together, eat together, lead together, and create success together.

Enjoy!

Chapter 1

Hungry

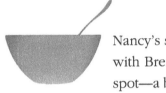

Nancy's stomach growled as she walked with Brenda toward their favorite lunch spot—a burrito joint with dirty floors, old furniture, and cheap, oversized burritos. After a long morning analyzing spreadsheets, reading reports, and engaging in heated discussions that lasted well into the lunch hour, Nancy was tired, hungry, and in need of food . . . quickly.

She didn't want to think about the bad news the spreadsheets revealed. She didn't want to worry about the reports anymore. And she didn't want to talk to one more person about the future of her company. All she wanted to do was eat. Yet instead of turning left into the burrito joint, she grabbed Brenda's arm and whispered, "Keep walking." Her intuition was stronger than her hunger, and it told her that the man with the mustache in the blue suit was following them.

"What's the matter?" Brenda asked, as Nancy began to jog instead of walk.

Nancy pointed and nodded toward the man following them.

"Again," Brenda said.

"Yes, again. Come on. Let's lose him," Nancy said as she grabbed Brenda's arm and they ran down the street. Moments later, they came to an intersection, turned left, made a quick right, and then took the next left, zigzagging their way through downtown, hoping to lose their pursuer.

The first time Nancy realized that someone was following her, a few months ago, it terrified her. She'd called her husband, a retired police officer, in a panic, only to learn at her board meeting later that day that it was probably some form of corporate spying. *More like idiot espionage*, she thought. She was told it came with the job of being the newly appointed CEO of a company that everyone was watching. With its stock price in the tank, revenue falling, and rumors swirling, the company was a likely acquisition target, which meant that business reporters, investors, potential acquirers, and powerful businesspeople were doing their due diligence on the company, and it also meant that they wanted to know more about the new CEO.

Her life wasn't in jeopardy, but her privacy was, and Nancy didn't like it one bit. She did whatever it took to keep the prying eyes out of her life, even if it meant forgoing mouthwatering burritos and running through downtown streets. Thankfully, her effort paid off, and when Nancy and Brenda stopped in the middle of the street and looked around, their pursuer was nowhere in sight. They had lost him, and now it was time to eat. But where?

Nancy noticed a long line of people at the end of the street, and as she and Brenda approached, they realized that these people were waiting to eat at a restaurant. Brenda looked up and read the sign on the building: GRANDMA'S SOUP HOUSE.

"Let's eat here," Brenda said.

"Are you serious?" replied Nancy. "We *make* soup. We live and breathe soup. We are surrounded by soup every day of our lives. Do you think I really want to eat soup for lunch? I've had enough soup."

"Oh, come on," Brenda said. "Where else are we going to eat? And besides, look at this line. It's almost 1:30 and the place is still packed. It must be good. Plus, they probably have sandwiches and salads, too."

"Fine," Nancy said, realizing that her hunger was getting the best of her. "But if it's not good, you're buying the burritos tomorrow."

"Deal," Brenda replied.

Chapter 2

Grandma's Soup House

The lunch line moved quickly, and before long they were ordering from a cute young lady who stood behind the counter. It was one of those fast, casual places where you place your order, receive a number, and wait at your table for someone to bring the food. The good news was that the place was clean, the people were nice, and the smell was amazing. The bad news for Nancy, however, was that they didn't serve sandwiches, wraps, or salads. In fact, they didn't serve anything except soup and bread.

Just great, Nancy thought, as she and Brenda ordered their soup and were handed an empty plastic soup bowl with their order number on it. The person working at the cash register told them to simply place the soup bowl at the edge of the table, with the number facing outward, and someone would bring their soup shortly.

In most restaurants, when they say the food will be out "shortly," it usually means a wait of 15 to 20 minutes. But in this case, the register person meant it. Within two minutes, a good-looking twentysomething with dark hair and blue eyes delivered their soup and bread with a big smile and a warm welcome.

"Have you been to Grandma's Soup House before? You look very familiar," he said as he stared at Nancy. He knew he had seen her somewhere before, but he couldn't quite place where.

"No, this is our first time," Brenda answered. "We sort of found it by accident."

"Well, I'm glad you did. My name is Peter. Just let me know if you need anything. I hope you enjoy the soup," he said before walking back to the kitchen.

"I'm sure we will," Brenda said as she smirked at Nancy, who ate her first spoonful.

The smell should have warned her. This was no ordinary soup. It was the best soup she had ever tasted.

"Well?" Brenda said, waiting for the verdict.

"Wow. I'm shocked," Nancy said, as Brenda also tried the soup.

"Yep, looks like I won't be buying burritos tomorrow," Brenda quipped.

"No, you certainly won't," Nancy countered as she attacked her soup with hunger and delight, savoring every bite. The soup was so good that Brenda and Nancy ignored each other until every drop was gone. They even wiped the bowl with their bread, hoping to savor the taste a little longer.

"You must have been hungry," Peter said as he approached the table with a big smile. "Did you enjoy the soup?"

"We loved it, as you can tell," Brenda said.

"Best soup I've ever had. What's the secret?" Nancy asked.

"My grandmother. She makes the soup every day."

"So, there *is* a real grandma behind Grandma's Soup House," Nancy said, nodding her head. "I like that. I thought the name was just some warm-and-fuzzy marketing ploy and Grandma was likely a 50-year-old bald guy with a mustache who smoked cigarettes in the kitchen while heating soup from a can."

"Oh, no," Peter replied. "Grandma is very real, and she's the reason I work here. I got my MBA from Cornell University, and just as I was graduating, she asked me to open this soup house with her. Fifty-fifty partners. I always thought I would go to work for some big company or head to Wall Street after business school. I was recruited by a number of Fortune 500 companies who wanted to develop me in their leadership programs but I found myself here, and I don't regret it one bit. In fact, I've learned more in the first six months working here than in all my years of schooling. Grandma is one smart lady. She knows more about business than you would think. In fact, she's in the kitchen. Would you like to meet her? You'll see how real she is."

Brenda and Nancy looked at each other as Nancy answered, "Sure." She knew they had a lot of work to do in the afternoon, but at the same time she was very curious to find out what made the soup so good.

Chapter 3

Grandma

When they walked into the kitchen, they spotted Grandma immediately. It was hard to miss her. The kitchen was small, and Grandma was not. She had a pretty face, a big smile, and every ounce of her radiated love.

"Hello, hello, hello. Who do we have here, Peter?" she cheerily inquired as she stirred a big pot of soup with a large wooden spoon.

Peter, realizing that the two women had never told him their names, wisely said, "I'll let them introduce themselves."

Nancy introduced herself as she approached Grandma with an outstretched hand, but Grandma wouldn't have any of it. She wrapped her big arms around Nancy, squeezed tight, and said, "Handshakes are for strangers. Hugs are for family."

Brenda, knowing she was next, approached Grandma and received a big hug, too, while introducing herself. It was clear that Grandma didn't know any strangers, because the minute you met her you became part of her family.

"So, did you like my soup?" asked Grandma.

"We loved it," answered Nancy. That's why we were excited to meet you and ask . . . " but before she could finish her sentence, Grandma cut her off and interjected joyfully "That's *wonderful*. I'm so glad! So, tell me about *you*. Tell me about your *family*." Grandma, who could tell she was a businesswoman by her fancy-schmancy suit, considered asking her about her business and work, but she was really more interested in the person behind the suit. Grandma knew that every person who went to work took not only his or her briefcase but also his or her childhood dreams, family, history, home life, and problems, too. Grandma wasn't interested in masks and facades. She wanted to get to the core of a person—and often did. She could learn more about someone in 10 minutes than most people could learn in 10 years. She disarmed people with her hugs, warmth, and smile, and Nancy, surprisingly, found herself opening up. She told Grandma about her two sons who played high school football, her seventh-grade daughter who loved to sing and dance, her supportive and loving husband who recently retired from the police force after 20 years of service, and her work as CEO of Soup, Inc.

"I know that company well," Grandma said. "When my kids were young and I didn't have time to make my own soup, I'd just open up a can of your company's soup. Now we're both in the soup business. Isn't that fabulous!"

"I knew I recognized you from somewhere," Peter said excitedly. "I've been racking my brain trying to figure out how I knew you. It was from the article I read about you in the *Times*. The article said you were trying to turn things around at Soup, Inc. I became a big fan of yours after reading the article. It's such an honor to have you in our restaurant."

"Thank you, Peter. I appreciate that. We're doing our best," she said, knowing in that moment it was time to go. "Brenda and I actually have to get back to work. We have a lot on our plate right now, as you can imagine." She turned to Brenda and motioned that it was time to leave. She thanked Grandma and Peter for their hospitality and delicious soup and said she'd be back. Grandma gave her a big good-bye hug and said, "I really hope you come back."

"I will," Nancy said, knowing in her heart she wasn't telling the truth.

Chapter 4

Nancy

As she and Brenda navigated their way back to the Soup, Inc., headquarters, Nancy wanted to kick herself for mentioning that she was the CEO of Soup, Inc. People treated her like a celebrity and a rock star, but she didn't feel like one. After all, just a few months ago, before the board chose her to run the company (and hopefully to save it), she had been the vice president of marketing. The board said her marketing team and campaigns were the one bright spot in the company and that she showed the leadership, innovation, and creativity the company needed. Although the board had confidence in her, she did not yet have confidence in herself. She had never run a company, never mind a company that was spiraling toward almost certain death. Once an icon of American business, Soup, Inc., had lost its way, and it was Nancy's job to help it find its groove again. Yet she didn't have a clue about what to do next. *Marketing*, she knew. *Advertising*, she knew. *Growing sales*, she knew. You could measure the success of marketing campaigns. You could see whether sales numbers were growing or declining. But the negativity and toxic environment that permeated Soup, Inc., was something she wasn't prepared to deal with.

When Peter mentioned the article in the *Times*, it merely reminded her of how lost she was. The article said that although she was putting a plan in place, the odds of it succeeding were almost nil. Nancy wanted to know the secret of Grandma's soup, but she didn't have time for more chitchat. She had to get back to work and figure out how to restore Soup, Inc., and get revenue growing again. She didn't plan to go back to Grandma's Soup House, yet she couldn't stop thinking about the soup. What made it so good?

Chapter 5

Another Bowl

The temptation to return proved too great, and as Nancy sat in Grandma's Soup House the next day, she thought about her long morning filled with conference calls, discussions, and ideas to increase sales. She had considered asking Brenda to have lunch brought in, but Grandma's Soup House kept popping into her head. She had to find out what made the soup so good, and besides, it was also a good excuse to enjoy another bowl. Brenda had wanted to come along, but she had too much work to do, and besides, Nancy thought Grandma would be more likely to reveal her secrets if she came alone. She promised Brenda that she would bring back a bowl of soup for her.

Nancy finished her soup, marveling at the number of people who stood in line waiting to eat. The line was even longer today than yesterday. Yet it moved quickly, and people didn't seem to mind waiting. Or perhaps they minded, but the soup was worth it. She watched as people in line smiled in anticipation of their order, started conversations with complete strangers, and excitedly explained the ordering process to the rookies who had never been to Grandma's Soup House before. The thought occurred to her that *great soup makes people happy and brings people together.* She pulled out her notebook and wrote this down. When she looked up, she saw Peter walking out of the kitchen. They made eye contact, and he walked over to greet her.

"It's great to see you again," he said. "I'm so glad you came back. Grandma is going to be excited that you are here."

"Does she have time to talk?" Nancy asked. "I don't want to bother her if she is busy."

"Oh, no, not at all. She's just making more soup right now, but she has time. We've been extra busy since that review came out in the paper. Looks like we'll have to make more soup each morning. All part of the growth process."

"I know what you mean," Nancy said, wishing her own company were experiencing a growth process.

"Come on back," Peter said as he walked Nancy to the kitchen.

Grandma gave Nancy another big hug. "It's so good to see you again!" she exclaimed warmly. "So, you couldn't stay away from my soup, could you?"

"Honestly, no, I couldn't. I couldn't stop thinking about it. The smell. The taste. The way it makes you feel."

"It has that effect on people," Grandma said, smiling.

"What's the secret?" Nancy asked as she looked around the kitchen and noticed a bulletin board with pictures of smiling children.

Grandma let out a big laugh. "Everyone always wants to know the secret. But it's not what you think," she said, wagging her finger at Nancy.

"So, what *is* it?" Nancy asked, hoping this wasn't the end of the conversation.

Grandma had an answer for her, but the secret had nothing to do with food.

Chapter 6

Who Stirs the Pot Matters

Grandma put her hand on Nancy's shoulder. "Everyone thinks it's the food, and, while I use the freshest ingredients around, so do a lot of restaurants. Others say it's the recipes. And, while my soup recipes have been in my family for generations, there's nothing special about the recipes. Sure, the recipes make tasty soup, but there are a lot of great recipes out there. The secret is *me*. Who stirs the pot matters," she exclaimed. "You can't separate the soup from the soup maker!"

"Why is that?" Nancy asked, trying to wrap her mind around what Grandma was saying.

"Because *you* are the number one ingredient in anything you make," Grandma said. "Whether it's a painting, a poem, a house, a business, or a pot of soup, the energy you put into it impacts your creation."

Grandma continued, "For example, did you know that some wine experts can determine the personality of a winemaker by tasting that maker's wine? There is a common challenge experienced by chefs that I call the 'stirring-the-pot phenomenon.' No matter how carefully different chefs follow the same recipe, the final product always varies a little bit. Even if two chefs do everything exactly the same way, the meal will always come out a little differently. Who stirs the pot has an impact on what's in the pot!"

Grandma's eyes sparkled with remembrance, "I also learned this truth as a young girl. My grandmother loved to cook, and to her, food and love were one and the same. When she cooked, she wasn't just making a meal. She was pouring out the love in her heart and sharing this love with her family. When we ate her food, we loved her back. And *no* food, no matter who makes it, ever tastes as good as hers did. Her love made the difference. And I believe it's this same love I put into my soup that is the secret ingredient. So, the secret is *me*."

"It's the same with our business," Peter added. "People always ask why our business is so good, and it's not just the soup. The same energy Grandma puts into the soup we put into our people and into our business."

"And this also applies to *your* business," Grandma said as she continued stirring the soup. "Whether we are making soup, managing a restaurant, or leading a big company like Soup, Inc., the stirring-the-pot phenomenon is the same." Then she said something so important that Nancy took out her notepad and pen and asked her to repeat it. Here's what Grandma said.

The love and energy we invest into our life and work determines the quality of it. The love we share in raising our children or developing employees or helping a customer impacts the final product. The love, or lack of love, we give ourselves and share with others will determine whether life is sweet or sour. It determines the fabric and texture of our relationships and how others perceive and receive us. When we love our kids, they feel it. When we stir the pot at work with love, our customers and colleagues notice. Just as soup is a reflection of the soup maker, our lives, careers, and businesses are the reflection of the love and energy that we put forth.

Grandma then stopped stirring the soup and put her hands on Nancy's shoulders. "Peter told me about the article in the *Times* and the struggles you are facing," she said, nodding her head reassuringly, "and you need to know something very important, and it is this. While your company has had other leaders stir the pot, they have never had *you* lead the way. The past is the past. The leaders before you made decisions that resulted in bad soup. But you can make new soup, and, remember, the most important ingredient is *you*. Who stirs the pot matters, and you, my dear, matter a lot."

Chapter 7

Teachers Are Everywhere

Nancy smiled. She knew everything Grandma said was true, yet she was surprised to hear such great advice coming from her. She was hesitant to talk about Soup, Inc., but she couldn't disagree with what Grandma was saying. In her heart of hearts, she felt she was different and could do a better job than her predecessors, yet her lack of experience as a leader frightened her. She asked herself a million times why she had ever accepted the job, but something had compelled her to do it. She had always believed that teachers are found everywhere, and she tried to learn from everyone she met. She considered herself a lifelong learner. It was a lesson she had learned from her father, who had been an NFL coach, and it was something she carried with her throughout her life. But she had to admit that the kitchen of a soup house was the least likely place she expected to find the solutions she sought—and Grandma was the least likely of teachers.

"So, how do you know so much about running a successful business?" asked Nancy.

Grandma laughed. "Oh, I don't know much about business. That's Peter's department. But I know about food. I know about people. I know about parenting. And I know about life. The same principles apply. Besides, I think if more people in the business world listened to their grandmothers, they would do the right things, and this would lead to success, not to mention a better world. Grandmas keep it simple. *Simple* is the key to success."

Nancy laughed. She couldn't argue with her. Grandma's business was packed, and her soup was amazing. Nancy's company, on the other hand, was losing customers and sales every day. Perhaps she was making it too complicated. Perhaps the answers *were* simple. Since she was the one responsible for stirring the pot, perhaps she just needed to figure out what to put in the pot.

"Okay," she said, looking at Peter and Grandma, "so, who stirs the pot matters, and I need to stir the pot. But what ingredients do I need to put into the soup to make it successful? I hear you saying that I'm the most important ingredient, but there has to be more."

There *was* more, but Grandma knew that Nancy had absorbed all she could handle for now. She knew the best way to make great soup was to add each ingredient one step at a time. Try to do too much at once, and you might as well pour the soup down the drain.

"That's a conversation for tomorrow, my dear," Grandma said. "I have a list of ingredients to share with you, but for now, I have to get back to my soup and you have to get back to yours. Here, take this wooden spoon as a symbol and as a reminder to stir the pot. Think about what we talked about. Think about how you can stir the pot. Come back tomorrow, and we'll start with the first ingredient every leader and every soup maker must share."

"And take this," Peter said nervously as he handed Nancy a piece of paper. "I hope you'll read it."

"What is it?" Nancy asked.

"Well, I've been thinking a lot about the challenges you are facing, and based on my culture and performance class in business school and the article in the *Times*, I wrote this and thought that you would benefit from it."

"I'll take a look at it. Thank you, Peter. And thank you, Grandma, for your insights," Nancy said as she walked out of the kitchen. She ordered a bowl of soup to go for Brenda and made her way back to the workplace, where the culture and the soup were rotting.

Chapter 8
Soup = Culture

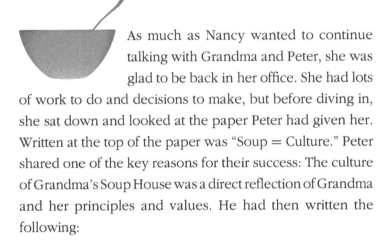

As much as Nancy wanted to continue talking with Grandma and Peter, she was glad to be back in her office. She had lots of work to do and decisions to make, but before diving in, she sat down and looked at the paper Peter had given her. Written at the top of the paper was "Soup = Culture." Peter shared one of the key reasons for their success: The culture of Grandma's Soup House was a direct reflection of Grandma and her principles and values. He had then written the following:

1. *Soup = Culture.* Just as soup is a direct reflection of the soup maker, so is the business culture a direct reflection of the leader. The soup and the culture at Grandma's were one and the same, and both were a reflection of *who* stirs the pot, as well as the values, principles, and ingredients the stirrer mixed into it.

2. *Culture drives behavior, and behavior drives habits.* Culture influences what your leaders and teams

think, say, and do each day. A lot of organizations focus on strategy and ignore culture, yet culture trumps strategy every time.

3. *Soft is powerful.* Many leaders think of culture creation as a warm-and-fuzzy, feel-good, *soft* project that isn't urgent because you can't quantify it with *hard* numbers. However, the most successful organizations know that although culture *seems* soft, it is really powerful and essential.

4. *You must nurture your culture.* Too many organizations aren't willing to invest the time and energy needed to create the culture they desire. They talk about culture, but they don't invest in it. Too many organizations focus on the fruit of the tree, such as stock price, costs, sales numbers, and revenue targets, yet ignore the root of the tree—their culture—and wonder why the fruit dries up. For great fruit, you must nurture the root. You must focus on creating a culture that will deliver the outcomes and fruit you want. Sure, you have to measure sales, costs, and outcomes, but these are merely a by-product of your culture, teamwork, productivity, and performance.

5. *Great leaders create great cultures.* As a leader, you must work really hard on creating the right culture

and consider it your number one priority. Culture affects motivation, and motivation affects productivity and performance. It all starts with culture, and the most important thing a leader can do is to create a *culture of greatness*.

Chapter 9

A Culture of Greatness

Peter's letter went on to explain that whether you are a small-business owner, a coach of a team, a manager, or the CEO of a Fortune 500 company, your biggest priority is to create an environment that fuels people and their performance. Best of all, the recipe is simple. As Grandma said, success is simple, and so is creating a culture of greatness. You just have to do it, and it requires only three principles:

1. You create a culture of greatness by expecting great things to happen—even during challenging times.

2. You create a culture of greatness by expecting your people to be their best. You don't settle for anything less than excellence.

3. You create a culture of greatness by coaching, training, and developing your team to be their best.

Peter wrote that although these three principles sound like common sense, far too many organizations and teams expect their people to be their best but they don't invest time and energy to help them be their best, nor do they create an environment that is conducive to success. They want great results, but they are not willing to do what it takes to create a culture of greatness that fuels performance and develops their people. Peter then encouraged Nancy to make a commitment to create a culture of greatness at Soup, Inc., which would be the key to turning the company around. He said it would be important to consider the following:

- Culture is something that can't be delegated to human resources or to a member of the leadership team. It has to be driven by a team leader who is committed to and engaged in the process.
- It requires a lot of work up front, but not as much work as dealing with the crises, problems, and challenges associated with negative, dysfunctional, and subpar cultures.
- While most organizations waste a lot of time putting out fires, you can spend your time building a great organization that rises above the competition.

Peter finished his letter to Nancy by saying that all of this would make more sense when Grandma shared the ingredients for making great soup. Nancy sat at her desk, shaking her head. No wonder he was recruited by so many companies. It was clear that Peter was a smart young man. Most of all, he was right. Soup, Inc., certainly didn't have a culture of greatness. It was more like a culture of failure and dysfunction. She knew what needed to happen. She just didn't know where to begin. And, with the board growing more and more impatient, she hoped she had enough time to figure it out.

Chapter 10

Nightmare

Nancy awoke the next morning drenched in sweat. She'd had a dream, and it replayed in her mind like a scary movie. She was back in high school at a track meet. Her race was about to start and she couldn't find her running shoes. She searched frantically for them, then noticed she couldn't find her running shorts, either. She heard laughter, and both panic and fear consumed her. *Hurry, hurry, hurry*, she told herself as she raced around the locker room looking for her shoes and shorts. The race was about to begin, and she wasn't ready.

What a crazy dream, she thought to herself as she hopped out of bed. Here she was, a grown woman with children of her own in high school, and this was what she was dreaming about. It reminded her of a dream she'd had a few months earlier, in which she'd been back in college and had had to take a final exam on a subject she didn't know anything about.

"Are you okay?" her husband asked.

"Yeah, I'm fine. Just a nightmare," she said as she walked out of the room toward the kitchen.

As she made the coffee, it occurred to her that perhaps it was more than just a nightmare. Perhaps it was a way to release her anxiety about the future of her company. She certainly didn't feel prepared to take on Soup, Inc.'s challenges. And, after reading Peter's paper, she knew she hadn't made the right initial decisions. Instead of focusing on culture, she had focused relentlessly on the numbers. She was obsessed with numbers, numbers, numbers. Her approach came from years in marketing and also from the stress of having the world and the stock market watching your every move.

She should have known better, though. Her father, whom everyone called Coach Ken, had taught her everything there was to know about creating a culture of greatness. Culture was the reason why so many players wanted to play for his football teams. He and his coaches created a culture that attracted the best talent, and it was no surprise that his teams won so often. It was also no surprise that other NFL teams with terrific cultures were consistent winners every year.

Nancy had experienced the power of culture in her home life as well. Her father had expected the best from her, but he'd also coached her and her sisters to be their best. He'd even given them a playbook to help them focus on being their best and bringing out the best in others. Now, as a mother, Nancy and her husband shared these lessons with their children and created their own culture of greatness as a family. She knew that family culture was the reason children either thrived or failed after leaving their parents' homes. Great family cultures helped children thrive as adults. The children weren't smarter or naturally more talented. They simply had grown up in an environment where they engaged in the right habits, learned the right values, and developed a strong work ethic. She also saw this in the corporate world, as businesses with the best cultures not only produced consistent results year after year, but also produced leaders that other companies wished to recruit and hire.

Yet, even knowing all this, Nancy had not applied these lessons when she took over as CEO. Tears rolled down her cheek as she realized that after her father's death, she had stopped applying a lot the lessons he had taught her. She had become harder on herself and colder toward others. She had allowed life and the worldview of others to get the best of her and knock her off balance. But now she was ready to change direction and set a new course. Instead of numbers, she was going to focus on culture. She was ready to stir the pot and create a culture of greatness. But she didn't yet know what ingredients to put into it. Hopefully, Grandma would have some answers for her before her company was ruined.

Chapter 11

Lead With Optimism

As Nancy sat at a table alone, enjoying her soup, Peter walked out of the kitchen with Grandma. "How are you, my dear?" Grandma inquired warmly as they approached, then gave Nancy a big hug before they sat down at the table with her.

"We're not going back to the kitchen today?" Nancy asked.

"No, not today," Grandma said. "I'm finished making my soup, and I'm also waiting for a friend of mine who is coming in for lunch. I'm excited for you to meet her. You're going to love her, and I know she'll love you."

Nancy looked around. She preferred to talk with Grandma in the kitchen, where they had more privacy, but the soup house was packed and buzzing with conversation and clanking spoons, which made it unlikely that anyone would overhear their conversation. Besides, she loved the energy of a crowded, loud dining room, and the table she chose in the back corner of the restaurant seemed private enough.

"So, did you read the paper I wrote?" Peter asked.

"Oh, I read it, Peter. And I thought a lot about it. You're one smart young man, and I agree with everything you said. You brought up a lot of points that I knew, but honestly had lost sight of. I stopped being able to see the forest through the trees, and I'm thankful you helped me to see again."

Grandma beamed. "I'm so proud of him," she said as she squeezed his cheeks.

"You should be," Nancy said.

Peter blushed. He couldn't believe that the CEO of Soup, Inc., was not only sitting with him in his restaurant but that she loved his advice.

"So, are you ready to talk about the first ingredient every leader and soup maker should share?" Grandma asked as she looked at Nancy.

"I'm ready," Nancy said.

"Okay, let's get started. Because I know you're here for more than just my soup," she wagged her finger. "The first ingredient, my dear, is *optimism*. When I'm making my soup, I expect it to be great every time. When I arrive here in the morning, I expect my business to be packed during lunch. When we first opened, people told me that it would take six months to a year before we would break even. I told them, no way. We're going to be busy the first week, and we were. When it rained, our employees used to worry that we would be slow, but I told them that what you expect, you get. I told them to expect it to be busy, and it was. Now when it rains, everyone expects our restaurant to be busy, and it is. The key to any successful business is optimism."

"It's really a competitive advantage," Peter said, joining the conversation. He wrote "Lead with Optimism" in big letters on a napkin and handed it to Nancy. The napkin looked like this:

In fact, the research confirms that optimistic salespeople outperform pessimistic salespeople. Optimistic leaders are able to garner the support of others.[1] And positive organizations outperform negative organizations.[2] Same industry. Two companies. The positive one will outperform the negative one.

---

[1] Martin Seligman
[2] Daniel Goleman

Chapter 12
Leadership Is a Transfer of Belief

"It's so true," Nancy responded. "I have found throughout my life that so often the difference between success and failure is belief."

"And do you believe you can turn your company around?" Grandma asked.

Nancy paused for a few seconds. "Honestly, I don't know. I can't say that I fully believe it."

"Well, honesty is a great thing," Grandma said, "because the soup doesn't lie. If you're not putting optimism into the soup, it will reflect that back to you. You can't hide it, and your team can't hide it. You have to decide what you believe, because if *you* don't believe, your people won't believe."

"She's right," Peter said. "After all, *great leaders share their belief, vision, and passion with others, and in the process they inspire others to believe.*"

He then wrote on a napkin:

"Do you know why I think beliefs are so important?" Grandma asked.

"Because of your restaurant?" Nancy said, shrugging her shoulders.

"Of course not," Grandma said, laughing. "I told you I know very little about business. I know this because as a parent, and as a grandparent, I have seen the impact by sharing my beliefs with my children and grandchildren. Whether you are leading a family or leading a company, the principle is the same. Great leaders transfer their belief to others. They are positively contagious."

Nancy knew this all too well. She had seen firsthand how great football coaches inspired their teams to win; she had seen how the great teachers in her life inspired her to believe in herself; and she had seen how her pastor had inspired the congregation to believe they could make a difference a world away in a tiny village in Africa. Not only had they raised money, but they had sent 20 volunteers and transformed the lives of the villagers. Positive beliefs lead to powerful actions, and Nancy had seen it happen too many times to chalk it up to chance.

Chapter 13

Guard Against Pessimism

"Remember, you're stirring the pot," Grandma continued, "and optimism must flow out of you so it can flow into others. Your team and company need your optimism and positive leadership more than ever. You are not just managing your people. You are managing their beliefs. Instead of being disappointed about where you are, decide to be optimistic about where you are going. When your folks talk about the challenges, then you talk about the opportunities. When others talk about why the company can't succeed, you give them every reason why it can. I can remember when my children were young adults and they faced a setback or challenge. I always encouraged them to work through it. 'Everyone gets knocked down. Everyone has bad days,' I told them. 'But optimistic people get back up and with their positive beliefs they create a positive future.'"

"But what if *I* believe and others on my team *don't* believe?" Nancy asked. "What if I'm optimistic and others aren't?"

"Great question," Grandma said. "But I'm not the one to answer this question. . . . She is," Grandma said as she stood up and hugged the woman who was approaching the table. "Hello, hello, hello, Joy, Joy, Joy," she said, as she and the woman squeezed each other. Nancy tried to figure out how well they knew each other, because with Grandma it was hard to tell. It seemed like everyone was a lifelong friend. "Nancy," Grandma said, "this is my old dear friend, Joy. And, Joy, this is my new dear friend, Nancy."

"Who are you calling old?" Joy joked, as they all laughed.

Joy and Nancy said hello to each other, as Peter pulled another chair up to the table for Joy.

Grandma explained that Joy is a bus driver who drives an energy bus, as Joy likes to call it, because she energizes everyone who rides on her city bus, and that after finishing her route, she often comes into Grandma's Soup House; from the first moment they'd met they had become instant friends. They shared a love of food, family, and people and would sit and talk for hours.

Grandma then brought Joy up to date on their conversation about optimism and reiterated Nancy's question about what to do if *you* are positive but your team isn't positive, to which Joy replied, "The way I see it, it's really simple. You invite people onto your bus. You share your optimism with them. You transfer your belief. You give them a chance to get on. You encourage them to be optimistic, but the fact is, you can't drive anyone else's bus. Some won't get on the bus. That's okay. If they won't get on, then you have to let them off the bus. The fact is, as pessimism rises, performance decreases. You have to encourage optimism and guard against pessimism, or your team will suffer."

Joy had shared this with many people in the past, and, while some didn't like it, everyone who heard it knew she spoke the truth—especially Nancy.

"Now it's up to you," Grandma said. "You must believe, and you must inspire your team to believe. It's not anything you haven't heard before. It's simple, but it requires action. Stir the pot with optimism and you will transform the soup."

Nancy liked what Grandma and Joy said so much that she wrote the following in her notebook:

As pessimism rises, performance decreases. You have to encourage optimism and guard against pessimism, or your team will suffer.

Chapter 14

The Mirror Test

That night, while her husband watched the game on television, Nancy read a business article titled "Positively Contagious." It said that the flu is not the only thing you catch at work. It turns out you are just as likely to catch someone's bad mood and negative attitude. The latest research demonstrates what we all know to be true—that emotions are contagious. Researchers call them *emotional contagions*, and they impact our work environments, productivity, teamwork, service, and performance in significant and profound ways. One negative employee can pollute the entire team and create a toxic work environment. One employee in a bad mood can turn off, and turn away, countless customers; and pervasive negative attitudes can sabotage the morale and performance of a team with great talent and potential. The good news is that *positive* emotions are just as contagious. One positive leader can rally a group of willing people to accomplish amazing things. One positive employee who sits at the welcome desk can positively infect every person who walks into your business, school, or workplace. Pervasive positive attitudes and emotions at work can fuel the morale and performance of your organization. You have a daily choice to be negatively contagious or positively contagious. You can be a germ and attack your organization's immune system, or you can act as a dose of vitamin C and strengthen it.

Nancy stood in front of the mirror as she brushed her teeth. *Which are you?* she asked her reflection. *Are you a germ, or are you vitamin C? Can you do this, or do you just want to give up now? Because if you don't believe you can do it and if you don't believe this company can be turned around, then you just might as well give up now. Why waste your time?*

The reflection stared back but didn't say a word. It was reaching into the deepest part of its soul, searching for an answer. Not an answer the person in the mirror wanted to hear, but the truth she deserved. She took a deep breath, said a silent prayer, and then the answer came. The woman and her reflection became one, and Nancy was filled with the belief and confidence that she could do this. She wasn't ready to give up yet. Her father had always told her that God wouldn't bring you to it if He weren't going to see you through it. She had used the mirror test when deciding whether to accept the job as CEO, and once again it told her she was on the right path. She believed she could turn around her company. Now, she just needed to find out who else believed and, more important, who didn't.

Chapter 15

Nancy Stirs the Pot

The soup doesn't lie. Grandma's words echoed in Nancy's mind over the next few challenging weeks as she executed her plan to stir the pot with optimism. She would also draw upon Joy's words as she sought to identify both the optimistic leaders, who would help Soup, Inc., become successful again, and the pessimistic naysayers, who needed to get off the bus. The first thing she did was unload a few of the pessimistic members of her leadership team. They were convinced the company was doomed, regardless of the actions they took. In their minds, they had already quit, even though their bodies went to work each day. They figured they would go along for the ride as long as they were collecting a fat paycheck. They had the skill but not the will. They had experience but no hope. They had become worn out like an old shoe. Nancy had struggled with the decision for a while, knowing that some of these people had been with the company a long time; yet they could not help to save the company, and now was the right time to let them go. It certainly wasn't easy, but the future of her company depended on it.

Next, she conducted a survey, asking employees to rate their managers and leaders in terms of optimism and pessimism. If she were going to be successful, she needed to surround herself with positive leaders and managers who would stir the pot with optimism in their respective departments. As CS Lewis wrote, "What is necessary is never impossible," and she needed people who lived by this. Positive energy flows from the top down in an organization, and if her leaders and managers weren't on board then she couldn't get the rest of the company on board, either. She knew that the leaders in an organization set the example for others. They must be examples of optimism.

Chapter 16

Hire Possibility Thinkers

Interestingly, for all the information the surveys provided, Nancy didn't need a survey to determine who was optimistic and who was pessimistic. Nancy knew exactly who fell into each category. While she and her leadership team waited for the surveys to come back, they met with every department manager and leader in the company. It took almost every hour in the day to accomplish this, and although she didn't get to see much of her husband and kids for a few weeks or visit Grandma's Soup House, it was well worth it. The surveys, her reports, and the reports of her leadership team matched up perfectly. There was a ton of pessimism in the company, and it started with a core group of negative managers who made life miserable and unproductive for their employees.

It wasn't easy, but Nancy and her team let them off the bus compassionately, providing a fair severance, transition counseling, and advice to help them learn and grow from their experience. Then, using a talent company, they focused diligently on finding the right optimistic people, both within and outside the company, who could lead, manage, and rally their teams. They weren't looking for yes-men. They wanted possibility thinkers, and these came in all personality types. They welcomed nonconformists who would contribute new ideas to help the company grow. They were okay with people who played devil's advocate, as long as their ultimate goal was to serve the team and deliver the best product to their customers. And they welcomed people who shared their ideas and complaints, as long as they were solution-focused. What they had to get rid of, however, were those who sucked the life and energy out of the company, those who sabotaged morale, and those whose negativity was contagious. The one ingredient she didn't want in her company's soup was negativity. Nancy told everyone point-blank, "The next time you head into work with a negative attitude, you might want to stop before you walk in the door and consider what your boss would say if you had the swine flu. He or she would tell you to stay home until you are healthy and not contagious. And in that moment, as you stand at the door, you have a choice: You can go home so you won't infect anyone, or you can choose to become healthy right then and there by changing your attitude and deciding to be positively contagious. You are not an island unto yourself. You are forever contagious, and you and your emotions and attitude impact everyone at Soup, Inc. So, come to work with a positive attitude or don't come at all."

Her number one priority was to build a team of optimistic leaders and managers who believed that they could change the direction of Soup, Inc. They were on the brink of survival, and it would take a group of optimistic people to make it happen.

Chapter 17

A Unifying Vision

When Nancy looked at the organizational chart, she felt a whole lot better about the future of Soup, Inc. She had assembled a team that was more energetic, more optimistic, and harder working than the previous team. No one creates success alone, and it would take this kind of team to accomplish what the naysayers said was impossible. She knew that great leaders build great teams, and she believed that the organization was finally on the right track. Yet she also knew it wasn't enough just to assemble optimistic people. You also had to give them something to be optimistic about. She had to create a positive vision for the future of Soup, Inc. She had to give her leaders and employees something meaningful and valuable to strive toward. It wasn't enough to tell them they were working to save the company. They needed to believe in something bigger than themselves—and she needed something to believe in, too.

She had Brenda do some research to identify the current mission statement of the company, because no one seemed to know it or remember it, and when Brenda found it in a file folder it was clear why. The mission statement took up an entire page and was filled with jargon and buzzwords that meant nothing to the people who read it. Not only was it too long to remember, but you wouldn't want to bother even if you could. Nancy threw the paper in the trash and knew they needed to start over. She wasn't looking for *War and Peace*. She wanted a unifying vision that everyone in her company could rally around. She had studied successful vision statements, and one of her favorites was IBM's "Let's build a smarter planet." Long before it was an advertising campaign, it was an internal rallying cry to mobilize all the employees to promote, sell, and service projects that built, served, and connected data systems to gather, analyze, and communicate information. With two words, *smarter planet*, everyone in the company knew it was their mission not only to create a smarter planet but also to create a huge success for IBM by making data more available, intelligent, and useful.

Nancy wanted a unifying vision statement like this for Soup, Inc., and it had to have the following five characteristics:

1. It had to be a vision everyone could rally around.

2. It needed to capture the essence and spirit of the business and to be something the organization could share with words and reinforce through actions.

3. It needed to remind everyone what Soup, Inc., stood for and to serve as the North Star that kept everyone on track.

4. It needed to be easy to remember by leaders and employees so they could live and breathe it every day. It couldn't exist only on a piece of paper in a filing cabinet. It needed to come alive in the hearts, minds, and actions of everyone at Soup, Inc.

5. It had to be clear, simple, energizing, and compelling.

Nancy shared the criteria with her leadership team as they met in a conference room for a vision brainstorming session. After a few hours of discussion and writing ideas on a big whiteboard, Carlos, who had taken over Nancy's job in marketing, shouted out the words that everyone agreed would be the company's new unifying vision.

Chapter 18

Spread the Vision

The words *Feeding Greatness* were not just two words that made you feel good. They were a call to action:

1. To feed yourself each day with the optimism and habits to be your best and accomplish great things.

2. To feed your team with great leadership and knowledge to help them be their best.

3. To feed your customers with great soup made by great people who work at a great company.

Nancy wasn't sure whether it was the perfect vision statement, but it was one that everyone at Soup, Inc., could rally around, remember, and live. She considered it one of her biggest priorities to share the vision statement and the essence of it with every leader, manager, and department in the company. She also decided that *vision* was another essential ingredient that needed to be added to the soup recipe, and she would surely tell Grandma and Peter about it when things slowed down and she could get back there for lunch. Until then, she had a vision to share. Over the course of the next few weeks, she spoke to every department and employee in the company, sharing and reinforcing that vision. She asked each leader, manager, and employee to think about what "Feeding Greatness" meant to them, and she received a lot of great feedback.

Nancy also added a big-picture goal to share along with the vision: "A can of soup in every house." While the vision itself captured the meaning and purpose that everyone could rally around, she also wanted to convey a big-picture goal that provided a tangible result the company could shoot for. "Feeding Greatness" was the company's North Star, but the employees also needed a goal toward which their North Star would hopefully guide them. "A can of soup in every house" represented the reason they were in business, the success they hoped to achieve, and it was another way of inspiring others to think big and act big. The company's thinking had been too small for too long and now it was time for a bold vision and bold goals. After all, if you are going to strike out, you might as well strike out while swinging for a home run. Even if Soup, Inc., were to have a can of soup in only 50 percent of households, it would still be the envy of every food company in the world. For the first time in a long while, Nancy and her team felt great about their soup.

Chapter 19

Build Trust

Nancy sat at her favorite table at Grandma's, eating her soup, reading the reports, and shaking her head. The numbers were improving, and progress was noticeable, but she thought the company would be much further along by now. She wasn't sure what she felt most: frustration or hopelessness. She had poured every ounce of optimism and vision she had into the soup, and while it was better, it still wasn't great. She was practically sleeping at the office, sacrificing time that could have been spent with her husband and children, and what did she have to show for it? A minor improvement in the growth of sales and productivity. The numbers still fell way short of where they needed to be to appease the board and save the company, and she wasn't sure what to do next.

When Peter saw Nancy, he came running over. "Grandma and I thought we scared you away," he said.

"Oh no, Peter, quite the opposite. You gave such good advice that I've spent the past month immersed at work, stirring the pot with every ounce of optimism I could muster. It's been the most challenging month of my life."

"Well, wait here," Peter said. He went into the kitchen, grabbed Grandma, and they joined Nancy at her table. Grandma, of course, gave Nancy a big hug and told her how much she had missed her. Nancy explained why she hadn't been back to eat and told them about the plan she had executed to let go of the pessimists and hire optimists. She also told them about the importance of adding vision to the soup, and Grandma and Peter agreed it was an essential ingredient—one that was essential to their business as well. In fact, Peter repeated the vision statement for Grandma's Soup House: *"To provide our team and customers the love, food, and service we would share with members of our own family."*

Grandma then asked Nancy whether sharing optimism and vision had made an impact on her business.

"A little. But not as much as I thought it would," Nancy replied. "I'm not quite sure why."

"It's simple," Grandma said. "You haven't added *trust* to the soup yet. As with any great recipe, certain ingredients are meant to complement one another, and optimism and vision work a whole lot better when trust is included in the recipe. Trust is your missing ingredient."

"How do you know this?" Nancy asked.

"Because if you had trust, you would have seen a bigger improvement by now. When it comes to trust, you need to know what my late husband Marty always said about trust during his years leading a clothing manufacturing business. I miss him terribly and can still hear him at the dinner table telling me the five things about trust that everyone should know." Grandma then proceeded to enumerate the following guidelines:

1. *People follow the leader first and the leader's vision second.* You can be the most optimistic person in the world and have the most inspiring vision, yet if the leader is not someone people will follow, the vision will never be realized.

2. *Trust is the force that connects people to the leader and his or her vision.* Without trust, there is a huge gap between the leader and the vision.

3. *If your team trusts you, and your optimism causes them to believe in you, then your vision will inspire them to follow you.* When leaders gain the trust of their team, then their beliefs, optimism, and vision are much more persuasive, and people will follow you.

4. *Trust generates commitment; commitment fosters teamwork; and teamwork delivers results.* When people trust the leader and their team members, they not only work harder, but they work harder for the good of the team.

5. *Trust is built one day at a time, and yet it can be lost in a moment.* The one thing in life you don't want to throw away is the trust people have in you.

Peter then shared a case study from his time in business school: A new CEO had decided not to make any changes during his first year, because first he wanted to build the trust of his team. After he had secured their trust, he enacted changes that were very successful.

"But I don't have a year," Nancy said anxiously. "What do I do to build trust?"

"First, find out how much or how little your employees trust their leaders and managers," Grandma said. "Then come back tomorrow and we can discuss a few more ingredients that will help you build trust. Okay, my dear?"

"Sounds like a great plan," Nancy said. She wrote down on a piece of paper the ingredients Grandma and Peter had shared with her thus far.

> Lead with <u>Optimism</u>
> Spread the <u>Vision</u>
> Build <u>Trust</u>

Then Nancy picked up her notebook and pen and made her way back to her office, pondering whether people had any trust in her at all.

Chapter 20
Busy

Kathryn, the vice president of customer service, walked in while Nancy was reading the results of the survey. "Do you have a minute?" Kathryn asked.

"Actually, I'm slammed," Nancy answered. "I have to read these reports and then I have a conference call with the sales team. We have to get sales going around here."

"I know," Kathryn said, trying to sympathize with her boss and, hopefully, engage her in a conversation. "It's just that I was hoping to talk about some ideas I have to improve our customer service operations."

"I'd love to hear them," Nancy said, barely looking up as she continued reading the reports. Although Kathryn stood right in front of her, she could have been on the other side of the building as far as Nancy was concerned.

"When would be a good time?" Kathryn asked, wishing her boss would look up.

"Just schedule it with Brenda," Nancy said, wishing Kathryn would leave her office so she could focus on her reports.

"Got it," Kathryn said. She walked out of the office feeling about as small as her customer service budget. Clearly, whatever Nancy was reading was more important than she was. *Maybe next time*, she said to herself.

Chapter 21

The Survey

The bad news was that the results of the trust survey showed that the company's employees didn't trust Soup, Inc. Years of mismanagement and a focus on rewarding lazy leaders, while at the same time overworking and mistreating employees, had led to a collective mistrust of the company. Not to mention the fact that the executive suite served as a revolving door. It seemed like every year, a new leader appeared who appointed a new leadership team and formulated a new direction for the company. Yet many of these leaders never stayed around long enough to do what they said they were going to do, and those who did stay ran the company and the culture into the ground. Why would the employees at Soup, Inc., trust the company when the company did everything to violate their trust?

The survey showed that while most of the employees shared Nancy's optimism and were excited about her vision, they nonetheless believed that either the company would be sold off before Nancy could accomplish her goals or she would leave for another opportunity. With this sinking-ship mentality, people at all levels of the company were more focused on their own survival, their own paycheck, and their own future than on the future of their team and the direction of Soup, Inc.

Nancy had to laugh at herself. How could she have missed this? It was so basic, and yet she had completely overlooked the importance of trust. Without trust, people wouldn't commit themselves fully to their team, to the company, or to the vision and goals she had set forth. Nancy and her leaders and managers needed to earn the trust of employees to get their commitment. But how?

Chapter 22

Enhance Communication

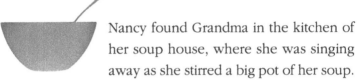

Nancy found Grandma in the kitchen of her soup house, where she was singing away as she stirred a big pot of her soup. She had a beautiful voice, and if Nancy had been in a better mood, she would have enjoyed listening to her. But Nancy was not in any mood to listen to singing or to eat soup. The results of the survey had kept her awake all night. She didn't have a year to build trust. At most, she had three months, and she could feel her goals slipping away. She was tired, her stomach was in a knot, and all she wanted to do was talk about how to build trust.

"Hello, my dear," Grandma said in between singing and stirring her pot. "Almost finished," she said as she bent over, put her face close to the soup, and took a big whiff. "The smell just brightens my day." Then she turned off the stove, covered the pot, and walked with Nancy to her favorite table, where Peter was already sitting.

"So, angel face, tell me what you found out." Grandma loved to come up with different nicknames for people.

Nancy revealed the results of the survey and the employees' distrust of the company. She explained that although people shared her optimism and vision, they thought she would leave like the other leaders before her, so they wouldn't commit.

Grandma shook her head while Peter wrote these words on a napkin:

Grandma and Nancy looked at the napkin.

"Yep," Grandma said. "Communication is so important. Communication builds trust, and it is key to any successful family or team. It's like I told my children when they were growing up. I said, 'Whatever you do, don't ever lie to me, because if you lie to me, then I can't trust you. And if we can't trust each other, we can't be a strong family. Communication is everything.'"

"I *have* been communicating," Nancy countered. "I've even visited every department and spoken to them honestly about the vision."

"That's great," Grandma said. "Obviously, that's why the survey says they share your optimism and believe in your vision, but now you have to communicate, communicate, communicate in a way that builds trust, not just rallies people toward a vision. The key is to fill the void."

Chapter 23
Fill the Void

Peter explained, "These are uncertain times for your people. They are wondering what's going to happen next. They're questioning how their job will be impacted. They're confused about what action to take. Unfortunately, this uncertainly creates a *void* in communication, and where there is a void, negativity will fill it."

Grandma added, "It's the same with marriages. Marriages go downhill when communication breaks down. Relationships fall apart when there is a lack of communication. That's because where there is a void of clear and positive communication, we start to assume the worst and act accordingly. Fear and negativity creep in and dominate our thoughts, behavior, and actions."

"This leads to a lack of trust, which leads to a lack of focus, teamwork, and success," Peter said. "Instead of taking positive actions to thrive, we go into survival mode and just try to survive. You must focus on building trust through frequent positive communication so that fear can't breed and grow. Communication builds trust, and trust conquers fear." Peter then wrote on a napkin:

Fill the void with positive and frequent communication.

Nancy nodded. She understood the importance of communication. It was the key to any successful relationship. It certainly was the key to keeping her marriage strong. Even though she and her husband were doing a million different things and running in different directions, they always found time to talk about their goals, their dreams, their relationship, and their children. Communication created a bond that helped them take on the challenges and distractions of a busy world. And it was this kind of bond that also built relationships in the workplace.

"What you are saying is so true. It is amazing," Nancy said, "that as companies we spend millions of dollars communicating and advertising to our customers, attempting to earn their trust, and yet we spend so little effort communicating and advertising to our most important customers—our employees. If we did more of this, we would trust ourselves more, and in turn our customers would trust us more. It starts at the core. So, how do I enhance communication, fill the void, and build this trust?" she asked, wondering whether Grandma and Peter knew something that she didn't.

Chapter 24
Add a Big Dose of Transparency and Authenticity

"First, it starts with you," Grandma said. "Remember, you are stirring the pot. You add a lot of communication to the soup and a big dose of transparency and authenticity with it. If you communicate in an authentic and transparent way, people will be more likely to trust you, believe in you, and follow you. Your communication has to be real and you have to be real."

Nancy knew this to be true. People were tired of leaders who read from a script and who asked questions based on some active-listening and management class they took. People didn't want to follow robots. They wanted to be led by real people who shared real emotions and who had real challenges. People wanted leaders and managers who spoke from the heart and who spoke the truth. She had an idea, and she told Grandma and Peter she was going to host a series of interactive meetings to eliminate as much uncertainty as possible and to enhance two-way communication; in this way, she could not only share information with her employees but also receive feedback from them.

"That's a great idea," Peter said. "But remember, it's not just you who has to earn their trust. All your managers must consistently fill the void with positive communication. It's essential that your managers also communicate one-on-one with the people in their departments. Trust is built one person, one relationship at a time. Your managers need to share the status of the company. They need to let people know where they stand. They need to listen to their employees' fears and needs and share a positive vision for the future, and they need to explain how you are positioned to help them get there. Your managers are key in building trust throughout the organization. If you always fill the void with positive communication at the organization level, the team level, and the individual level, then negativity and fear can't breed and grow. And if you are transparent and authentic in your communication, even the cynics will trust you. They may not agree with you, but they will trust you."

It sounded simple, but Nancy knew that it wouldn't be simple to get every leader and manager in the company to build trust through communication, transparency, and authenticity. She needed a simple way to explain this to her leaders and managers that would help them take action. Grandma had an answer, but, as expected, it had nothing to do with business.

Chapter 25

Treat Them Like Family

"How do I get my leaders and managers to understand the importance of this?" Nancy asked.

"Well, you do what we do here," Grandma said. "You encourage them to treat their team members like family."

"That's a little clichéd, don't you think?" Nancy had heard that too many times in the business world, only to see the promise unfulfilled.

"Well, let me clarify," Grandma said. "Treat them like a *functional* family. The difference is trust and love. In functional families, people trust one another and care about one another. Sure, they fight and have disagreements like most people, but the trust and love keep them together. In dysfunctional families there's no trust, love is not put into practice, and therefore the disagreements break down the bond. Functional families communicate a lot with each other. They are open and honest with one another. They are transparent and authentic. They trust one another. And they share their love with one another," she said as one of their employees walked over to say good-bye to Grandma and Peter. She had to leave work early to attend an afternoon college class and Grandma gave her a big hug good-bye.

Grandma then sat back down and continued, "So the message of treating them like a functional family speaks volumes, and it's one that almost everyone can understand and relate to. Best of all, seeing people as members of your family changes the way you treat them. You see them as people who deserve your trust and love and who require communication, transparency, and authenticity from you. You want to be someone they can trust, and therefore you take the actions necessary to earn it. You say what you are going to do, and you do what you say. And you do it all with love."

Chapter 26

Love

As Nancy walked briskly back to her office, she thought about what Grandma had said and noticed that love kept coming up in their discussions. Grandma talked about stirring the pot with love and loving your people like members of your family. It was obviously the most important ingredient in making great soup, and it was something her father had talked a lot about as a coach. In the old days, he would say, you could yell at people and achieve success by instilling fear. Not anymore. Today's athletes were more interested in having a relationship with their coaches, and most of all they wanted to know you cared about them. Nancy, too, had observed this growing trend in the business world and had taken many seminars that discussed how younger generations were redefining the workplace and leadership in a good way. They didn't just want to work somewhere. They wanted to create a life within their jobs. This meant having meaningful relationships and interactions with leaders who communicated with them with transparency and authenticity.

It occurred to Nancy that the number one question her team members and employees were asking was, *"Can I trust you, and do you care about me?"* In fact, it's the number one question we're all asking of each other in the world. If people know that they can trust you and that you care about them, then they will follow you to the ends of the earth. Yet Nancy wasn't sure how to apply this at work. Treating employees like family, while a lofty goal, was difficult to put into practice. She knew from experience.

When she arrived at her office, she pulled out her notebook and added ingredients to her list for making great soup.

> Stir the pot with Love
> Lead with Optimism
> Share the Vision
> Build Trust
> Fill the void with positive Communication
> Add a big dose of Transparency and Authenticity

Chapter 27

Rumors

For Nancy, the hardest part of being a CEO was not running the company or enhancing the communication of her leaders and managers. For her, the hardest part was dealing with all the rumors and subtle negativity that where swirling around the company. There were rumors that Nancy would be replaced. There were rumors that another company would be buying Soup, Inc. In fact, every day it seemed there were new rumors of a takeover by a different company. Fueling the rumors, financial news shows ran segments speculating how long Soup, Inc., could last on its own. Nancy knew she couldn't control the media monster. It came with living in a world dominated by a 24/7 news cycle. She viewed the media as the "bible of the fearful," always focusing on doom and gloom and always highlighting the worst in people, not the best.

She knew there was no way she could control what the media said and did. There wasn't a manual to guide CEOs on navigating the specific set of circumstances she was dealing with. However, she could control her own actions and the way she ran her company. People were entitled to their opinions, and they would always be more than happy to share them. Then, after sharing them, they would move on to formulate other opinions, while Nancy and her team would focus on what they could control. She shared this message with her teams and made sure she addressed the false rumors about her company. Her communication was frequent, transparent, honest, and real. This made a big impact, and the employees began to trust her more than the rumors they heard. She found that people couldn't assume the worst if they weren't given the opportunity to assume. She replaced the assumptions and uncertainty with truth and facts via daily e-mails, company-wide conference calls, weekly meetings, and status updates. She filled the voids with positive communication. She also noticed a big improvement in communication from her managers and their departments. She told them that now was not a time to remain in their offices: "You can't manage from your office, so walk the floors, visit with people, talk to them, address their concerns, and remind them of the vision we are all striving toward." The managers heeded her advice; they focused on building trust through enhanced communication, and it became clear to everyone in the company that things were on an upswing at Soup, Inc.

It became clear to everyone except the board, that is. Unfortunately, the board concentrated single-mindedly on the spreadsheets and the numbers, which showed only minimal improvement. The numbers didn't reflect all the positive changes that were happening behind the scenes.

By focusing only on the numbers, the board members couldn't see the collective optimism that was brewing. They weren't aware that communication had significantly improved morale. They weren't aware that productivity was on an upswing. Most of all, they couldn't see all the progress Nancy had made with culture. She knew a lot of great things would materialize from these efforts, but outsiders couldn't see it because it wasn't measurable, and this really frustrated her.

However, what Nancy didn't realize was that you *could* measure the progress they were making. It just required a new measuring stick, one she was about to find out how to use.

Chapter 28

A New Measuring Stick

Nancy's father had always told her that great leaders don't have all the answers. Rather, they surround themselves with people who are smarter than they are and who help them find the answers. That's why Nancy had hired Brenda. Brenda was more than her executive assistant. She was a Harvard MBA who planned to run her own company one day. She was only 30 years old, but she had a lot of experience and knowledge, and she wasn't shy about sharing it with Nancy. During the turnaround, Brenda shared a lot of valuable ideas, but nothing was more valuable than the information she shared on employee engagement.

She eased Nancy's frustration at not being able to measure the company's progress by letting her know that there was indeed a useful measuring stick. It wasn't an exact science, but it had been used by a large number of companies, and there was a lot of evidence to show that *engagement* was the measuring stick Nancy was looking for. For years, companies such as Gallup had been measuring the engagement of millions of employees for countless organizations. For example, Gallup uses a 12-question survey, called the Q12, whereby employees, based on their engagement score, are classified into one of the following categories:

1. *Engaged.* Employees are energized by their work and the mission of the company.

2. *Not engaged.* Employees have quit before they quit. They're at work but not working with energy or passion.

3. *Actively disengaged.* Employees aren't just miserable. They are also sucking the life out of their team and organization.

Brenda further explained to Nancy that companies are able to analyze the survey results to connect their overall engagement scores to worker performance. In other words, the more engaged your employees are, the greater their performance, which leads to sales growth, enhanced productivity and innovation, better customer loyalty, and other indicators of higher performance. Engagement surveys are also used to determine an organization's ratio of *engaged* to *actively disengaged* employees (which is an indicator of an organization's health). Gallup, through its extensive research,[3] has found:

---

[3] http://www.gallup.com/consulting/52/employee-engagement.aspx

- In average organizations, the ratio of engaged to actively disengaged employees is 1.5 to 1.
- In world-class organizations, the ratio of engaged to actively disengaged employees is nearly 8 to 1.

"It's really simple," Brenda said. "If we want to be a world-class organization, then that means for every eight people in our company who are energized about working here, there should be only one person who is sucking the life out of the company."

Finally, Brenda shared that Gallup's research demonstrates that engaged organizations have 1.6 times the earnings per share (EPS) growth rate compared with organizations in the same industry with lower engagement. This was music to Nancy's ears, and it would also be music to the board's ears if Nancy could demonstrate that Soup, Inc., was engaged and moving in the right direction. Even the board could see the importance of these numbers.

Nancy armed herself further with numerous case studies that Brenda shared detailing the success organizations had achieved by focusing on engagement. These organizations were able to track engagement scores over a number of years, and they could literally correlate their engagement scores to sales growth and profit.

Nancy was excited. She had always loved numbers, and now she had a number that truly meant something. By measuring the engagement of her company, she could paint a picture of not only where Soup, Inc. was but also

A New Measuring Stick

where it was going. She could predict future success by the relative engagement of the employees and the company. She could use engagement scores to determine whether she was succeeding in her efforts to create the right culture. Grandma said the soup doesn't lie, and engagement presented a powerful and meaningful way to measure how well she was making the soup.

This brought up an important point that Nancy and Brenda knew had to be addressed. It wasn't enough just to measure engagement. After measuring it, they had to put together a plan to enhance it, then execute the plan at all levels of the organization. So, what would be the best way to increase engagement? Hopefully, she would find out at Grandma's Soup House.

Chapter 29

Relationships

When Nancy walked into Grandma's Soup House, she heard the employees behind the counter call out, "Welcome to Grandma's!" Clearly, this was a group that was engaged by their work. When she asked Grandma and Peter what they knew about engagement and how to enhance it, she wasn't surprised to hear that Peter was well versed in the concept and that they used their own informal way to measure their engagement ratio. With only 20 employees, it was easy to figure out whether they had an 8 to 1 ratio of engaged to actively disengaged people. However, Peter and Grandma used their own terms for identifying engagement:

- *Hot*, for someone who was engaged
- *Lukewarm*, for someone who was disengaged
- *Cold*, for someone who was actively disengaged

Grandma shared that, to her, engagement was all about relationships and treating people like family. "Relationships are the ingredient that gives life and work meaning, flavor, and texture, and they are necessary to create great soup."

"Relationships are everything," Peter added. "Although this seems like common sense, believe it or not, there's an effort by a lot of managers and leaders in the business world to keep the professional and personal separate; but the fact is that relationships in the workplace *are* personal, and they are necessary if you want to enhance engagement and create success. Think about it. Gallup's research shows that employees who think their managers care about them are more loyal and productive than those who do not think so. Employees who have a best friend at work are more engaged. Other studies show that the biggest determinant of employees' decisions about whether to leave or stay in their jobs is their relationship with their manager or boss. It all comes down to relationships. You need to have great relationships with your team if you want to build a winning team." Peter then summarized what they had discussed over the past few days about trust, communication, love, and relationships.

Communication, trust, and love create the foundation for any successful relationship. Without communication, trust, and love, your relationship won't be very strong; and without strong relationships, you can't have a strong team; and if you don't have a strong team, then you can't have a strong organization. Relationships are the foundation upon which winning teams and organizations are built.

Chapter 30

Soup Is Meant to Be Enjoyed Together

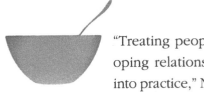

"Treating people like family and developing relationships isn't so easy to put into practice," Nancy said, thinking about her own schedule and the demands on her work and personal life. "I can't even seem to find the time to have a relationship with my own husband and kids, never mind relationships at work."

"Developing relationships sure isn't easy," Grandma said. "Relationships take time. They take effort and commitment. And I have to be honest. I'm afraid in today's world that we're so busy with work, career, to-do lists, technology, multitasking, and projects that we are forgetting the importance of relationships. We spend more time talking online to people we don't know than to our own neighbors. We live in our homes as strangers, not taking the time to develop a relationship with our kids. And our kids are too busy online and on their phones to talk to their parents. They are living distracted lives, staring at their text messages rather than looking at the people in front of them. And at work we're so busy trying to create success that we forget to develop the relationships necessary to create success."

Grandma was on a roll: "We need to get back to basics and remember that it is the relationship that is the ingredient and foundation for great families, great teams, and great organizations. Humans were made for relationships, and soup is meant to be enjoyed together. We must invest in each other and in building relationships. As my Marty always said, 'The quality of your business and life is determined by the quality of your relationships.' And while great relationships are founded on trust and love, it also works the other way. Through relationships, you build trust and share love more powerfully. When you make relationships your priority, your life and work will be so much more enjoyable and meaningful, not to mention easier."

Chapter 31

Rules Without Relationship Lead to Rebellion

"When I think about what Grandma just said," Peter added, "I think of Andy Stanley's quote. He said that 'rules without relationship lead to rebellion.' So many managers focus on the rules they want their people to follow, but without relationships, people are not motivated to follow them."

Nancy interjected, "It's the same with coaching. My father was a coach, and he always told me that the key to his success was that he took the time to get to know his players and develop a relationship with them. He had a lot of rules, but the players loved him, so they followed them."

"It's the same with parenting," Grandma added. "When you take the time to be with your kids and grandkids," she said as she put her arm around Peter, "and nurture your relationship with them, they are much less likely to rebel against the rules you have set forth." Peter then wrote on the napkin again for Nancy and Grandma to see:

> To effectively lead and develop someone, you have to have a relationship with them. It is through relationships that you can shape people to be their best.

"That's wonderful Peter," Grandma affirmed warmly. "I would also add to that and say that all transformation requires a relationship. We are transformed through our spiritual relationship with God and our relationship with family, mentors, and coaches, and we transform others through our relationships with them. Only through relationships can we transform and be transformed."

Chapter 32

The Enemies Are Busyness and Stress

That night, Nancy jogged around her neighborhood with her dog while her sons were at football practice and her husband took their daughter to dance practice. As she jogged, she was suddenly struck with an emptiness and sadness that stopped her in the middle of the road. She felt she'd been convicted by Grandma's and Peter's words. She realized she was one of the guilty ones. For years, she thought people should have their relationships *outside* of work, not *at* work. In fact, before Brenda, she couldn't think of one person she considered a friend at work. She believed in her marketing metrics and numbers and had shied away from getting too close to anyone—especially after her father had died. She had forgotten the lesson he taught her, not with words but in the way he coached and parented. He had built winning teams because of the relationships he developed, and he developed a winning family because his relationship with his kids was his number one priority.

Although Nancy did the same with her kids, she hadn't been spending much time with them lately. She planned to change this very soon, as soon as Soup, Inc., was running smoothly again. Thankfully, they were still a strong family, and it was because of the bonds they created. She knew these were the kinds of relationships that she and the leaders and employees at Soup, Inc., needed to develop with one another at work if they were going to transform the organization. She also knew that the process had to begin with her. She thought about the day Kathryn had come to her office, how she had barely even acknowledged her. No wonder Kathryn had never followed up to share her ideas. Why would she? Nancy hadn't taken the time to connect with her and earn her trust.

It was clear that she had made some mistakes. Since she took over Soup, Inc., Nancy had focused primarily on numbers, numbers, numbers. She was too busy and too stressed to think about other people. She certainly didn't make time for relationships with her family or her leaders, and she had been so stressed that she'd almost missed out on developing a relationship with Grandma and Peter—a relationship that was changing her life.

She decided that the enemies of great leadership, great parenting, great coaching, and great relationships were definitely busyness and stress, and these obstacles were something she and her teams would have to overcome to build the relationships necessary for enhanced engagement and great teamwork. She was overwhelmed with work, and so were her managers. They had a ton of tasks on their plate, but for now they needed to focus most intensely on their soup and the relationships that would make it great. After all, when it comes to building a successful business, it's not the numbers that the drive the people, but rather the people and relationships that drive the numbers. Creating those relationships and developing that teamwork had to be their top priority.

Chapter 33

Engaged Relationships

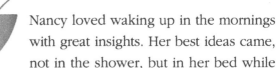

Nancy loved waking up in the mornings with great insights. Her best ideas came, not in the shower, but in her bed while she slept. She would often wake up in the morning with a great idea waiting for her. It was as if the idea waited for her to wake up, and when she did, bam, it would pop into her head. She could trace many of her most successful marketing ideas to these wonderful morning revelations, and this morning she was presented with another gift, consisting of two words: *engaged relationships*. She heard the words loud and clear and was energized by their significance. *It's not enough just to build relationships*, she told herself as she looked in the mirror. *We have to build engaged relationships*. Peter had been wrong. Relationships were not the foundation for building winning teams and organizations. *Engaged* relationships were the foundation. The culture and employee engagement at Soup, Inc., would be enhanced by focusing on engaged relationships. Nancy then went through a series of thoughts and steps in her mind, putting together the ingredients for great soup.

Optimism and vision start the process. They energize people with the vision and goals of the organization. But to reach these goals, the employees of Soup, Inc., needed to be engaged, and to be engaged, they had to develop engaged relationships. As a leader, she needed to encourage this, and her managers and employees needed to focus on it. Communication, trust, and love create the foundation of a relationship, and then you strengthen the relationship by engaging it.

Nancy had a lot of ideas, and she couldn't wait to discuss them with Peter and Grandma over lunch.

Chapter 34

Encourage, Inspire, Empower, and Coach

When Nancy walked into to Grandma's Soup House, she received her welcoming cheer from the employees, ordered her soup, and walked back toward her table, where Grandma was sitting. Nancy sat down, and a few minutes later, after helping his employees, Peter joined them. Nancy could hardly control her excitement.

"It's not just about relationships," she said. "It's about *engaged* relationships."

"I like that term," Peter said. "I never heard it before."

"I know. It came to me this morning."

"What does it mean?" Grandma asked.

"It means that the relationship is not a noun, but a verb."

"You lost me," Peter said.

"It means that relationships aren't stagnant. They are something we create every moment of the day, and it is our actions and the things we do with one another that engage the relationship and strengthen in it. Relationships are the result of the time we spend together, the interactions we have, and the work we do together. When I take a walk with my kids and talk to them, I'm engaging them and creating an engaged relationship. When I'm collaborating with a coworker, I'm engaging the relationship. Through our interactions and actions together, we develop the relationships and teamwork that enhance engagement, performance, and results. What I'm trying to figure out and hope that you can help me with is this: What are the best ways to engage the relationship?"

"Well, my dear," Grandma said, "now we come to the point where it's time to give the soup a little kick. What you are talking about is strengthening your relationships, and to do this, you have to add the ingredients of inspiration, encouragement, empowerment, and coaching to the soup."

Peter then added, "Having spent a lot of time reading case studies about this and working with the employees here, we've found that the best ways to engage your people is to inspire, encourage, empower, and coach them. And doing this not only benefits you and your relationship with them but also benefits the organization. Let's face it, everyone in your company contributes to the culture of it. Your people are not just a creation of your culture but are creating it every day. They must be encouraged, inspired, and empowered to stir the pot as well, and they must be coached so they are good at it."

"And you can't stir someone else's spoon," Grandma added. "You have to inspire, encourage, empower, and coach them to stir their own spoon."

Then Peter wrote on a napkin:

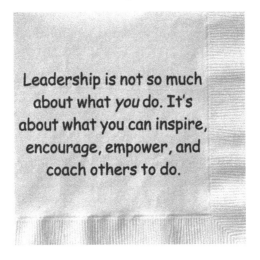

"I couldn't agree more," Nancy said. "But how do I inspire, encourage, empower, and coach them?"

"Well," said Grandma, "like any family, first you create an environment that allows empowerment to flourish, one where people feel and act empowered. This is what we do here at the Soup House."

Peter added, "Then you inspire, encourage, and coach them in this empowered environment so they can be successful. You get to know your people, because how can you lead and coach them if you don't know them? You have to know their strengths to help them develop their strengths. Then you spend time and collaborate with them, because only through shared experiences can you truly forge a connection with someone. Once you have this connection, then you will have the trust and relationship that will allow you to help them thrive. A relationship is necessary to effectively coach someone, and by coaching and encouraging that person, you also strengthen the relationship. And, of course, a big part of all this is creating a clear line of communication so that inspiration, encouragement, empowerment, and coaching can take place."

"Tell her how to create a team of pot stirrers," Grandma said as she patted Peter proudly on the back.

"Sure," Peter said, knowing that what he was about to say was not based on theory but based on his experience managing employees at the Soup House.

Chapter 35

A Team of Pot Stirrers

"Well," Peter said, "once you create a clear line of communication, you meet with each member of your team like we did here. In your case you also want each manager to meet with their teams."

During this meeting you and your managers want to reinforce the bigger vision you have created for the organization. Then you want to ask each person to create a personal vision and identify how he or she, with that vision, can contribute to the bigger vision of Soup, Inc. Then you must also ask them how you can help them achieve their personal visions and help them contribute to the bigger vision."

Peter continued, "By taking these steps, instead of just one pot stirrer with one spoon, you create a team of pot stirrers all stirring the pot with a shared vision and purpose. This generates a tremendous amount of empowerment momentum in the organization. Each person comes to work knowing how he or she can contribute to the team and organization. This energizes the team members and causes them to share positive energy with everyone they work with. Leaders may set and share the vision, but it is the positive energy of your people that will make this vision a reality. So you need to make developing a team of pot stirrers your priority. And once you have your team all making great soup, then you have to make sure you keep communicating with them, keep encouraging, keep inspiring, and keep developing their talent. It's not just enough to ask them how you can help them realize their vision. You also must make sure you actually help them."

"Such as mentoring and training," Nancy said.

"Exactly," Peter said. "It takes more investment up front but it pays dividends."

Then Grandma added, "If you want people to be their best, you must give them your best. Also when you invest in them, train them, and give them your best, this lets them know you care about them. Empower them and develop them and you will engage them. Help them be their best, and they will give you their best."

Nancy was inspired by the conversation and was filled with hundreds of ideas to inspire and empower her team and create engaged relationships. She just hoped there would be enough time to implement them.

When she arrived at her office, she added a few more ingredients to her list.

Stir the pot with <u>Love</u>
Lead with <u>Optimism</u>
Share the <u>Vision</u>
Build <u>Trust</u>
Fill the void with positive <u>Communication</u>
Add a big dose of <u>Transparency</u> and <u>Authenticity</u>
Create <u>Engaged Relationships</u>
Combine <u>Inspiration</u>, <u>Encouragement</u>, <u>Empowerment</u> and <u>Coaching</u>

Chapter 36
The Offer

The look on the board members' faces was not good, and neither was the news. Some of the rumors turned out to be true, after all. Another company had made an offer to buy Soup, Inc., and the board was strongly considering it. Nancy didn't know what to say. She was in shock. Sure, she had always known it was a possibility, but she didn't expect it to happen, certainly not like this and not for such an inadequate amount of money. It was almost laughable that the board members would consider such an offer, but in their view, the numbers weren't climbing fast enough and they had very few options left.

"You're panicking," she boldly told the board.

"We're not panicking," a director replied. "We simply have no choice."

"Yes, you do have a choice," Nancy countered. "You can let me continue to turn this company around and not act out of desperation."

"We have every reason to be desperate," said another board member. "The numbers aren't showing the improvement we need to see."

"You're focusing on the wrong numbers," Nancy challenged. "We're moving in the right direction, and even though the sales numbers don't show it yet, they will."

"What makes you so sure?"

"We have a new measuring stick. We're focusing on engagement, and as you can see from these charts of other companies that have focused on engagement, you can correlate an increase in revenue, profit, and stock price to an increase in engagement scores."

Several of the board members lifted their heads for the first time. She had piqued their interest.

"I'm not interested in a quick sale," she said. "I'm interested in building a company for the long term, and if you sell now, we're going to miss out on all the profits that will come our way in the future."

Nancy continued. "Just give me 90 days to show results and I guarantee that, within a year, it will be worth seven times the offer we have on the table. And in two years, it will be worth 20 times as much. If I'm wrong, then you don't have to pay me a salary."

"If you're wrong, you won't have a salary, because someone else will be in your position," said a board member.

"But if *you're* wrong," Nancy said, "and you sell this company, you'll never know what could have been. You'll always wonder *what if*. You can sell this company and be part of one of the worst business decisions of our time, or you can be part of one of the greatest corporate turnarounds ever."

She knew she had convinced them. They didn't know whether she could do it, but they couldn't say no to her. Nancy explained that they would measure engagement at the start and at the end of 90 days. She predicted that during this time the company would show an increase in engagement and, as a result, would see significant progress in sales. The board agreed to give her 90 days to show improvement. As she walked out of the meeting room, she took a deep breath and covered her face with her hands. She had put her future and the company's future on the line. Now it was up to her and her teams to either back up her words or eat them.

Chapter 37

Another Shot

"Move your feet," Nancy shouted to herself.

"Come on, Nancy, keep it going," Steven said.

She hadn't played tennis in months, but today she needed to hit some balls. She usually preferred playing on the weekends with her husband or at night with her kids when they didn't have other activities, but today she had to hit tennis balls during her lunch hour. Her sanity required it.

"I like the way you're hitting today," said Steven, her instructor. "Very aggressive. A break from the courts has been good for you."

If he only knew, Nancy thought. One by one she smashed each ball that came her way. Wham. Wham. Wham.

She wasn't just hitting balls. She was slamming the comments of the board members. She was crushing their smirks. She was punishing their doubts. Better to let her frustration out on the tennis balls than on people at work. Wham. Wham. Wham.

Each swing released some of her anger, stress, and frustration. She was naturally fiery, and it was one of the things her husband loved about her, but sometimes the fire needed to be controlled and she found tennis was a great way to do it.

After Nancy had hit a few bad shots, Steven stopped the rally and walked toward the net. "Keep your eye on the ball," he said. "Just focus on the ball. Stop thinking about the last shot." That's the great thing about tennis. If you hit a bad shot, you get another chance to make your next shot a great one. You just have to have a bad memory. The previous shot is gone. Just focus on making your next shot great. Each swing represents an opportunity to hit the ball the right way.

As Nancy walked off the court, drenched in sweat, she realized the past was the past. The board had given her another shot, and it was up to her and her people to make it great.

Chapter 38

40 Days of Engagement

Later that afternoon, Nancy gathered her leadership team, and they brainstormed ways to create engaged relationships, enhance engagement in every department of the company, empower their people, and, of course, grow sales. Together they created an action plan they called "40 Days of Engagement," which included a series of strategies and steps that would enhance communication, build trust, share optimism, and empower and coach people to do what they do best every day.

Over the next 40 days, they were on a mission, and they implemented a number of successful initiatives. The training department created Soup University and rolled out a program to every employee that focused on best practices to enhance engagement and build teamwork. Brenda was put in charge of creating a leadership institute within the company that would promote leadership practices and develop leaders from within the company. The leadership institute would also be responsible for improving the management practices of managers and those in leadership positions.

One of the initiatives Brenda implemented right away was to create an advisory committee of people selected by their peers whose assignment was to meet and develop a *Winning Habits* document that would promote acceptable habits and discourage unacceptable habits in the company. This was designed to create a more positive culture and an environment that would fuel performance. For example, desired habits included smiling at your coworkers when you passed each other in the halls and sharing encouragement; unacceptable habits included complaining without offering a solution (the "No Complaining" rule) and being rude to a colleague or customer. Because the winning habits were created by their peers, employees responded to them in a positive way, and they had an immediate impact.

To enhance relationships, Nancy and her team also launched a mentoring program. Nancy believed that everyone should be both a mentor and a mentee. This would strengthen not only relationships but also individuals. To stress the importance of this concept, Nancy herself became both a mentor and mentee, and she chose Kathryn as her mentee. No longer would she be too busy to invest in a relationship with her employees. Leaders lead by example, and she had to set the standard.

Chapter 39
No One Eats Alone

As a way to bring people together and create an interactive culture of greatness, Nancy also encouraged and launched a program to enhance communication and relationships, which she called "No one eats soup alone." She told her employees that soup was meant to be shared, enjoyed, and created together and that together they would accomplish great things. As part of the initiative, leaders and managers encouraged employees to have lunch with someone from a different department each week so they could brief each other on their challenges and accomplishments. Here again, Nancy led by example: She took a different person to lunch at Grandma's Soup House each week and also made it a habit to eat in the cafeteria with the employees. It was amazing how much information and how many ideas she gathered by breaking bread with her teams.

To further enhance communication and transparency and spread optimism, she shared a daily message via e-mail, conducted a daily 10-minute teleconference with the entire company, provided frequent status updates via the new company intranet, and hosted numerous town hall meetings. She became a proponent of positive and frequent communication and encouraged her managers to do the same. In turn, not only did the managers become a source of top-down information, but they listened a lot and implemented a number of improvements that came from the bottom up. Nancy and her team also shared critical financial reports and engagement numbers with everyone in the company, letting them know where the company stood and where it needed to be to reach the goals set forth. She told everyone about the results-oriented 90-day window of grace, and, as a result, everyone felt a shared responsibility for saving the company. They no longer felt like mere employees. They now felt as though they had some ownership.

Although saving the company and showing measurable progress was the short-term goal, Nancy knew it couldn't be their only source of inspiration. With an eye on the big picture, she continually shared the vision of "Feeding Greatness" everywhere she went. People had their goals, but they needed a North Star to guide them.

Chapter 40

Success Fridays

Nancy knew it was also essential to continually cultivate optimism and create a collective mind-set that expects great things to happen. To foster this, Nancy had every department, including sales, implement Success Fridays. This meant that every Friday, teams would gather in person or via webcam and share their success stories for that week. Nancy found that by focusing on success each week, her teams looked for, expected, and thus created more success. By sharing success stories, people learned from one another and improved their individual and team performance.

Each week, Nancy and her team would highlight these success stories via e-mails, phone calls, and the intranet. Employees no longer shared stories of failure and despair. They no longer complained to one another about how miserable their jobs were and how awful the company was. They were no longer merely soup producers. Now they had become pot stirrers. Instead of stories of defeat, they told stories of triumph, saving the company, helping a customer, making a huge sale, creating a better process, developing a new solution, or promoting an innovation. As their focus and stories changed, so did the company. Performance and productivity improved. Collaboration and teamwork increased. Engagement scores climbed. And, best of all, sales grew. After 40 days, they were on their way, but they still had a long way to go.

Chapter 41

Fill Up with Appreciation

It had been weeks since Nancy had sat down with Grandma and Peter. While she still had lunch at the soup house with Kathryn and various employees, her focus was more on spending quality time with her employees than on talking with Grandma and Peter. They would say hello and ask how things were going, but beyond small talk they didn't engage in their usual spirited and informative discussions. But today, Nancy showed up alone. With 50 days left to show positive results to the board of directors, she was sure some ingredients were missing in her soup, and she hoped Grandma and Peter would have some answers.

When they joined her at her favorite table, Nancy shared how the company had just finished her 40 days of engagement initiative. The sales numbers were up, people were excited, trust was at an all-time high, engagement had climbed significantly, and relationships had been strengthened. Yet she was still concerned. She had 50 days remaining, and teamwork and overall performance were not where she had expected them to be. Grandma asked her to explain all the initiatives implemented so far, and Nancy went through them one by one.

"I think I know what is missing," she said, wagging her finger. She had a certain look on her face. It was the "Grandma knows best" look that comes from living a long life full of challenges and lessons learned.

"You're missing the ingredient of *appreciation*. But here's the great news," Grandma offered enthusiastically. "It's one of the easiest ingredients to add to your soup, and it requires only two simple, powerful words."

"Two words?" Nancy asked curiously.

"Yes. They are two words that have the power to transform our health, happiness, relationships, and success. Of course, I'm talking about the words *thank you*." Peter wrote "Thank you" in big letters on a napkin.

"She's right," Peter said. "On a personal level, research shows that grateful people are happier and are more likely to maintain good friendships. A state of gratitude and appreciation, according to research by the Institute of HeartMath, also improves the heart's rhythmic functioning, which helps us to reduce stress and think more clearly under pressure—especially in stressful business situations. It's also physiologically impossible to be stressed and thankful at the same time, so appreciation and gratitude help you to counter the stress that gets in the way of cultivating great relationships. When it comes to building a great team and an engaged workforce, gratitude and appreciation are essential for a healthy work environment. In fact, the number one reason people leave their jobs is because they don't feel appreciated."

A simple thank-you and a show of appreciation can make all the difference.

Chapter 42

The Ultimate Recognition Program

Grandma then added, "So, ironically, while your leaders and teams are working so hard to implement all your engagement initiatives, you need to make sure you engage and recognize them with these two simple, powerful words. Make sure you offer a sincere 'thank-you' to as many people as possible during a given day. Walk up to your managers and say, 'I appreciate all you are doing during these tough times.' Tell them, 'You are very important to this company and to your team, and we couldn't save this company without you.' Let them know that you appreciate them. Make sure your managers are doing the same, and encourage team members to appreciate one another. We do it here every day, and it makes all the difference."

"It's the ultimate and best recognition program there is," Peter said. "One thing we studied in business school was the impact of recognition programs, and although companies spend a ton of money on them, most of them don't work as intended. They aren't sincere, nor do they motivate people in the long term. Purpose, meaning, self--reward, and genuine appreciation are the real driving forces behind great work. You can have a much bigger impact and save a whole lot of money by simply sharing your appreciation."

Wow, Nancy thought to herself. Here she had been thinking the answer had to be complicated, but once again Grandma had revealed a simple solution. It was so simple that she and too many others had overlooked it. The key, however, was to take the simple and put it into action. She knew what she had to do. "I can't thank you both enough," Nancy said as she got up from the table, hugged Grandma and Peter, and walked toward the front door. It was time to head back to work, but she was thankful to have gotten exactly what she came for. Before she walked out of the restaurant, she turned to Grandma and Peter and said, "I just want you to know how much I appreciate you. *Thank you* for everything!"

"We appreciate you, too, angel face," Grandma said as Nancy walked out the door.

Chapter 43

Great Service

The next day, while eating at Grandma's Soup House, Nancy looked at a card Kathryn had written her.

Dear Nancy,

I just want you to know how thankful I am that you decided to mentor me. Honestly, a few months ago I was planning to quit. No matter how much I needed the job and the paycheck, I could no longer work at place where I didn't matter. I hated coming to work and even worse I hated the person I had become while working here. But then everything changed. You stopped ignoring me. You started taking me to lunch. You gave me advice, and you listened to my ideas. For the first time I felt like someone at work cared about me and the work I do. Now I love coming to work. I feel like I'm making a difference, and I love taking care of our customers. It's all because of you. So thank you for making me feel like I matter. Thank you for making Soup, Inc., a place I love. I look forward to helping you and the company accomplish great things.

—Kathryn

Nancy placed the card on the table, wiped the tears from her eyes, and realized that her business was not much different than Grandma's Soup House. The key to both their successes was great leadership and great service. Although she wasn't serving food in a restaurant, she was in the service business; she needed to serve her people and in turn they would serve their customers. She decided that *great customer service begins with serving your employees first and your customers second.* If you shower your employees with appreciation, love, and respect, they will in turn shower your customers with appreciation, love, and respect.

Too often, businesses focus all their energy on satisfying the needs of the customer while ignoring the very employees who serve those customers. This approach may prove successful in the short run, but eventually employees become tired, burned out, negative, and resentful—they come to feel used.

Businesses that delivered legendary service also had the strongest, most supportive cultures in which employees were valued, listened to, cared for, served, appreciated, and loved; in turn, these employees valued, cared for, served, appreciated, and loved their customers.

"Great service begins with us," Nancy wrote in her notebook. "If we model it, our employees will live it."

Chapter 44
Leading by Example

Inspired and energized by Kathryn's card, Nancy heeded Grandma's advice and added a big dose of appreciation to the soup. She made it a habit to write three to five thank-you notes every day to the employees and customers of Soup, Inc., and encouraged her leaders and managers to do the same. She also wrote thank-you notes to her husband and children for being so loving and supportive. Before long, she and her managers had written hundreds of thank-you notes, and, as a result, engagement scores continued to climb.

Yet despite all their efforts and focus on engagement, communication, training, mentoring, and appreciation, there remained some people, like Tom and Claire, who were not engaged at all. There were some people who, although not overtly negative, weren't excited about working at Soup, Inc. They were, as Grandma would say, *cold* (meaning disengaged), and with only 30 days left to convince the board not to sell the company, Nancy knew she had to do something about these disengaged employees. There was still one more ingredient she needed to add in order to make the soup *hot*.

Chapter 45
Friday Night

Nancy loved going to her sons' Friday night football games. Even as a kid, she could remember being either in the stands or on the sidelines while her father played and coached football. He had been an all-American in college, a Pro Bowl player, and Hall of Fame coach in the NFL. Although her father was no longer with her, Nancy felt his presence most strongly at football games, and she knew he would have loved to watch her sons play. They had his talent, size, and fire.

She also loved going to their games because it offered a great escape from work. She immersed herself in the games and yelled so loudly that her sons had asked her to lower the volume a little. She never brought her work to the games, yet on this particular Friday night she discovered something at the game that she would take back to work.

While watching the players give every ounce of their energy on the field and observing the coaches as they paced, yelled, and cheered on the sidelines, she found the ingredient she needed to add to make her soup *hot*. She'd always heard that *organizations* don't change—*people* change. Changed people then change the organization. Cold people wouldn't do it. She needed *hot* people who would create *hot soup*.

Chapter 46

Passion

Nancy needed people who were hot with passion. Passion was the ingredient that would take them to the top. Passion was what she had noticed on the football field. The players and coaches had it, and her company needed it. When she arrived home that night, she wrote a memo that she would share the next day with the entire company:

> If we as a company are going to feed greatness and build a world-class company, then we need to infuse passion into our soup and into each other. This means that we must be a company that is filled with passionate people. In the past, you could be lukewarm and mediocre and still be successful. Not anymore.
>
> Now, in today's competitive environment, your passion and your purpose must be greater than your challenges. To be successful you have to be willing to work harder, learn more, practice longer, lead better, smile more, and love deeper, and this requires passion.

Passion wakes you up 30 minutes earlier. It dials your phone one more time to make one more sale. It rallies your team together when times are tough. It moves you to see one more customer after a long day. It inspires you to help a struggling colleague. It provides legendary customer service. Passion transforms workplaces, powers champions, and fuels winning teams.

"What about someone who has a low-paying job or who is in a job that, quite frankly, is hard to be passionate about?" you might ask. I've been thinking a lot about this, and it's not the job or the money you are being paid, but rather, it's the passion you bring to your job that matters. After all, I've met bus drivers who are more passionate about their jobs than professional athletes making millions of dollars. I've worked my way up in countless jobs, and I was as passionate about stocking shelves as I am about being CEO of this company.

Sure, I realize that not everyone is going to be passionate about all their daily responsibilities associated with their job. I'm certainly not passionate about everything I have to do each day. However, in these cases, you can focus on the one aspect of your job that you are passionate about. You can be passionate about the organization you work for. You can be passionate about your team members and helping them improve, grow, and succeed. You can be passionate about your mission and customers. You can be passionate about making a difference.

To all those in this company who feel they aren't able to express their passion because they are in the wrong position and would rather do something else, at Soup, Inc., I want you to be honest about this. We will do everything in our power to find a role or position in the company that allows you to use your gifts and strengths to serve our company with passion. And, if there are no jobs that you are passionate about at Soup, Inc., and you are meant to do something else, that's okay, too. We will do everything we can to help you find another job with another company that allows you to express and live your passion. This is good for you and your future, and it's also good for us.

Working somewhere else to live your passion will help you thrive, and it will also make room in our company for those who are passionate about Soup, Inc.—and with an organization filled with passionate people we, too, will thrive.

Nancy then had a meeting with all her leaders and managers and made it clear that they were to infuse passion into their teams. They were to hire passionate people, and they were to help people find their passion within the company or, if necessary, outside the company. Their passion had to be greater than their challenges if they wanted to succeed, and passion would be the key to take them to the next level. Not just for the next 30 days, but for the rest of their lives.

Nancy inspired her managers to help everyone on their teams to find their passion, adding, "If they aren't sure what their passion is, then encourage them to think about their purpose." Nancy knew that people are most energized when they are using their strengths and gifts for a purpose beyond themselves. Passion flows from purpose; therefore, in living your purpose, you will live with passion. "And if people aren't sure what their purpose is," Nancy continued, "then encourage them to think about their legacy. Why? Because *knowing how they want to be remembered helps them decide how to live today, and leaving a legacy will give them a purpose that will unleash their passion.*"

She also told them that passion had to come from within. "You can't stir someone else's spoon. They have to stir their own spoons. And, as a manager, if you are working harder on your employees' success than they are, then you have to let them go." It was tough love, but tough love would help everyone be the best they could be. Nancy's dad had always told her that people needed to be pushed out of their comfort zones to be their best, and she and her leaders would push everyone to give 100 percent.

Lukewarm wasn't an option. Cold soup was gross. Hot soup was the answer.

Chapter 47
Hot Soup

Over the next 30 days, the soup wasn't just hot—it was *smoking*. Nancy's memo was very well received, and people responded by working with more passion than ever. What she said was the truth, and everyone knew it. Also, because Nancy had been walking the walk and sharing her own passion, she had moral authority. She wasn't viewed as a hypocrite who said one thing and did another. She lived and breathed everything she said. Most of all, because she and all her leaders and managers had spent so much time communicating and building relationships and investing in their people, their people trusted them. When they practiced tough love, people knew it was because they cared about the company, not because they were out for their own interests. Because they had developed engaged relationships, people were more likely to follow their rules. Nancy realized that trust and likability were funny things, because two leaders could mandate the same exact rules, and yet people would be more likely to follow and accept the rules of the leader they liked and trusted most.

Although everyone trusted and liked Nancy, not everyone stayed at Soup, Inc. Some people (Tom, Claire, and about 20 other employees) left, and that was okay. They were obviously meant to find their passion somewhere else and were just taking up space. "It's the benefit of building a culture of greatness," Nancy told Brenda. "When you build the right culture, you don't have to kick people off the bus. They will get off themselves because they just don't fit in."

Nancy also made it clear that being passionate doesn't mean you have to be bouncing off the walls and cheering at your desk. People expressed their passion in different ways. Some displayed passion quietly. The key was that each person's passion about their job, their team, and the company would be reflected in their work and in the results. Nancy pulled out her notebook and added *appreciation* and *passion* to her list of ingredients.

> Stir the pot with Love
> Lead with Optimism
> Share the Vision
> Build Trust
> Fill the void with positive Communication
> Add a big dose of Transparency and Authenticity
> Create Engaged Relationships
> Combine Inspiration, Encouragement, Empowerment, and Coaching
> Fill up with Appreciation
> Heat with Passion

Chapter 48

Tastier Soup

As Nancy awaited the board meeting that would decide her future and the future of Soup, Inc., a funny thing started happening. The company started getting phone calls and e-mails from customers asking what had changed in the soup recipe. Countless customers reported that that the soup tasted better. They asked whether the company had improved the recipe and, if so, why it wasn't noted on the can. However, Soup, Inc., hadn't change the recipe at all. The company used the same equipment, the same ingredients, and the same process. "The only thing that has changed," Nancy told the employees on a conference call, "is *us*. We've changed. We are the most important ingredient, and our love, our passion, and our teamwork have made the soup even better."

While some employees thought it was just coincidence, Nancy knew there was more to the story. She theorized that there's a spirit, an essence, a core radiated by a great company's culture that persuades customers to choose its product on the shelves or to frequent its stores. Certain companies had it. Certain brands had it. Certain people had it. You couldn't explain it or quantify it. It was one of those mystical things you couldn't analyze with tools, but you knew it existed. There's a physical world and a spiritual world, and what is unseen is more powerful than what is seen. For years, Nancy had been buying a certain brand of milk without thinking twice about it. After Nancy met the milk company's CEO and learned more about the company's culture, it became apparent that there was a hidden determinant and unseen power behind her decision. It wasn't the carton design or price. It was company and the people and the mission behind the milk that appealed to her beyond her five senses. For the same reason that "who stirs the pot impacts what's in the pot," people were now saying their soup tasted better. When employees love their company, this is reflected in the marketplace, and, in turn, customers love the product. And now this was taking root at Soup, Inc.

Nancy decided that the greatest sales strategy of all was to create a great culture filled with engaged people who are passionate about the company they work for, the work they do, and the product they sell. This would create a brand that resonated with customers, which would lead to sales growth in the marketplace.

The directors were about to make their decision, and while Nancy couldn't control their decision, she was proud and confident of the fact that they had created the kind of culture that was making their soup taste better to their customers. If the board made the right decision and allowed

Nancy and her managers to continue building their company and culture, she and her team would continue to create the kind of energy that would lead to even more cans of soup flying off the shelves.

Culture not only drives behavior and habits, but it also drives sales.

Chapter 49

The Decision

Nancy's dad had always told her that the best of the best expect to win. Whether they are walking onto a football field, entering a tennis court, or filing into a sales meeting, winners expect a great outcome. Her father's words echoed loud and clear as she walked into the boardroom. It was D-day, decision day, and Nancy was expecting a great outcome. She had lunch brought in from Grandma's Soup House, hoping the aroma and taste of the soup would lift the spirits of the board members—even the ones who didn't seem to have a pulse or a spirit. The board members smiled as they ate the soup and read the reports.

"Amazing soup," said one of the board members as he looked at Nancy and Brenda.

"It's from a great soup house downtown," Brenda said.

Another board member chimed in, "I'm not saying our soup isn't good, because it is very good, but I have to say, this is some of the best soup I've ever tasted."

A third board member agreed, "If we sold this soup, we wouldn't have a worry in the world."

Nancy smiled, knowing that great-tasting soup wasn't the *only* secret to a company's success, although the directors' excitement about Grandma's soup did give her an idea.

"Enough about our lunch," the chairman of the board said. "I'm more impressed with the numbers Nancy has presented to us. Sales are up. Engagement scores have increased substantially. Costs are in line. If these trends continue, we could have our first profitable quarter in a long time. So, do you think you can sustain this?" the chairman asked.

"I do," Nancy said.

"How can you be sure?" one of the more pessimistic board members asked. This one loved to play devil's advocate, but Nancy had a lifetime of practice dealing with people like him.

"Oh, I'm very sure," Nancy said with a big smile. "Let's just say I've found the secret recipe to making great soup."

The board members looked at each other and smiled. They didn't know whether she was serious, but it was clear that the growth in sales and the company's improved performance were very serious.

Whether they were convinced by the numbers or by Nancy's confidence that the growth was sustainable, the board unanimously voted not to sell the company or accept any further offers. Soup, Inc., was officially off the market, and the financial reporters and business shows would have to find another punching bag. From now on, Soup, Inc., would be a story of success, not dysfunction.

Chapter 50
An Offer They Couldn't Refuse

"So, how'd it go?" Peter and Grandma asked Nancy, who sat across the table from them.

"Better than you can imagine!" she exclaimed. "We're officially off the market, and now I can continue building this company. We're going to launch a "We Are Family" engagement campaign to keep the momentum going. We're going to update the label designs on a number of our soups. We are going to focus on increasing shelf space in our stores. And, most exciting of all, we are going to add a new line of soup."

"What will it be called?" Peter asked.

"I was thinking of a simple name," Nancy said, "one that would conjure up a warm and cozy feeling and convey 'homemade' to our customers. How does 'Grandma's soup' sound to you?"

"I love it," Grandma said. "But what kind of soup will it be? It has to be good."

"Oh, it will be very good," Nancy said. "It will be the best soup anyone has ever tasted."

Peter and Grandma looked at each other.

"Yes," Nancy said, nodding, "I want to license *your* soup, and let's just say that, in doing so, Peter won't have to worry about paying for his kids' college education."

"First, I have to find someone to marry," Peter said, blushing.

"Oh, that will come, young man. I have a feeling you won't be single for long."

"You can't mess with my recipes," Grandma said as she wagged her finger.

"We won't," Nancy assured her.

"And I personally have to show your people how to make it. I know you have those big machines," she said, wagging her finger again, "so we need to make sure the quality can be maintained when making such large batches."

"You can do all the quality testing you want," Nancy said. "I wouldn't put your name on a bad pot of soup. After all, you're the reason why Soup, Inc., has a future. I can't thank you enough. This is one of the ways I want to say thank you, and, honestly, I think it's going to benefit our company a whole lot to have your soup on the shelves . . . not to mention all the people who will get to enjoy it."

"I didn't save your company," Grandma said. "Peter and I just shared the ingredients with you. You are the one who put them together."

"Well, I couldn't have done it without you. And now I want to continue building the company with you. After all, you are not just friends to me anymore. You are *family*," Nancy said with a big smile. "So, what do you say?"

Grandma and Peter looked at each other.

"Okay, it's a deal," Grandma said as she stood up and gave Nancy a big hug.

"Of course," Peter said, "I just want to see the terms of the contract."

"I wouldn't have it any other way," Nancy said. "I'll get the contract to you, and I'm confident this deal will be a win-win for all of us."

"In that case, I agree, too," Peter said with a big smile. He knew his future was bright. Now he just needed to find someone to enjoy it with.

Chapter 51

The Power of Relationships

Nancy walked back to Soup, Inc., headquarters thinking about all the marketing potential associated with Grandma's soup. Six months ago, they'd been strangers, and now, after a fruitful relationship that helped Nancy save the company, they were going into business together. She thought of all the turning points in her life and realized that every great event happened because of one relationship or another. She had met her husband through a relationship. She had landed her first job out of college because of a relationship. She'd been hired at Soup, Inc., because of a relationship. She reasoned that the people we meet and the relationships we develop have the biggest influence on the course of our lives.

It was a lesson she wanted to impart to her kids and anyone who would listen: "The world is a mosaic of people and opportunities, and when you make relationships your priority, the possibilities are endless. Great relationships lead to great outcomes. Develop as many great relationships as possible. Make time for them. Nurture them.

Engage them. Not just at work but at home. In your community. On airplanes. At the ball field. Everywhere. You never know where your next idea, opportunity, or life--changing moment will come from or which relationship will be behind it."

Chapter 52
Unity

Fast-forward three months: Nancy looked around the ballroom. She was hosting a company-wide event to celebrate the success of Soup, Inc. She and her teams had implemented the "We Are Family" engagement campaign a week after the board meeting, and, as a result, sales and profits continued to grow, as did morale and engagement. Nancy had worried that once they had saved the company, people would go back to their old ways, but that hadn't happened. With a unifying vision and commitment to creating a culture of greatness and engaged relationships, everyone in the company focused on continuous improvement, day-by-day, month-by-month, quarter-by-quarter. They didn't focus on how good they were, but rather on how much better they could become. This focus, drive, and passion permeated the culture, and Nancy knew they needed this celebration to honor their hard work and efforts.

It wasn't your typical company event, however. Instead of inviting only employees, Nancy invited the employees' families, too. Her dad had always told her that unity was the difference between an average team and a great team, and unity meant being one family. It wasn't enough to have just the employees on board; real unity and engagement came from having the employees' families on board as well. Everyone, including the employees' families, contributed to their culture and had a role in stirring the pot. While many leaders tried to separate personal life from business life, Nancy knew the line was blurred. One impacted the other.

During the company celebration, she presented awards and recognized people not only in front of their peers but also their families. She shared the vision, numbers, and goals. She described where the company stood, how far it had come, and where it was going. She believed that if the spouses and significant others knew the numbers and also bought into the vision, they would be more supportive of their spouses' work—especially when they had to travel or work overtime. Having the support of their families would make employees feel even better about their work and even more engaged. Instead of being united at work and divided at home, they would be one family, all stirring the pot together to create a culture of greatness, and this unity would take them to even greater heights.

To reinforce this message, while giving her closing remarks, Nancy had her leadership team and managers hand out a wooden spoon to every employee and every family member. She reminded everyone that to be a great company they needed everyone in the room to stir the pot. If they did it together and poured their heart and soul into making great soup, they would accomplish amazing things.

Toward the end of the evening Nancy looked across the room and saw Peter and Brenda talking to her husband and children. Peter, in addition to running Grandma's Soup House, became a consultant for Soup, Inc., and was instrumental in developing the training program for and teaching at Soup University. As part of his job, he worked with Brenda quite a bit, and they realized they shared a love of business and soup. Nancy chuckled to herself as she observed Peter and Brenda holding hands as they spoke to her husband and kids. Yes, indeed, Soup, Inc., really was becoming one family, and together they were making great soup.

She looked at her phone and noticed an e-mail came in from her travel agent. She looked forward to her upcoming vacation with her husband and kids. They were heading to an island with no phone reception, no e-mail, and no distractions. She had worked really hard to nourish her work family, and to be truly successful, she knew she also needed to nourish her husband, her children, and her own soul.

Chapter 53

The Recipe Book

Three months later Nancy walked into Grandma's Soup House holding a stack of books. Over the past year, she had posted on a big bulletin board in her office all of the ideas Peter had written down on napkins. She had also posted her own thoughts and inspirations, as well as insights that came from Brenda and other employees. Eventually, her office was practically wallpapered with the ingredients, principles, and suggestions for creating great soup. One day she decided to take all the ingredients, all the strategies, and all the ideas implemented at Soup, Inc., and publish them in a recipe book—with Peter's help, of course. It was not to be a recipe book for making actual soup—but rather, it would be a recipe book for nourishing your team and culture.

She gave copies of the book to every employee at Soup, Inc., and planned to distribute them as well to every MBA program where she was a speaker. Her turnaround of Soup, Inc., had become legendary, and she was frequently invited to deliver keynote addresses at business conferences and universities detailing her recipe for success. Nancy welcomed the opportunity to discuss her company's turnaround and hoped that her story—and the recipe book—would help others overcome their own challenges and construct their own triumphs.

However, in every talk she gave and in her recipe book, Nancy shared a disclaimer that knowing the recipe and ingredients wouldn't guarantee success. Anyone could memorize the recipe and ingredients. The real art was in putting the recipe together. And along the way, it would be essential for leaders to refine the recipe, to tweak it to fit their own culture and tastes, and to add additional ingredients as they saw fit. Each person would ultimately have to create their own recipe for success, and Nancy hoped her recipe book would serve as a guide to do this.

Nancy handed a stack of books to Peter as Grandma beamed with pride. When Grandma opened one of the books, she especially liked what Nancy wrote on page 1. It said, in big bold letters:

Who stirs the pot is the most important ingredient in the soup. Just do your best and stir the pot with love!

For ideas and strategies to initiate your own engagement program visit:

www.soup11.com

A Recipe to Create a Culture of Greatness

Stir the pot with Love

Lead with Optimism

Share the Vision

Build Trust

Fill the void with positive Communication

Add a big dose of Transparency and Authenticity

Create Engaged Relationships

Combine Inspiration, Encouragement, Empowerment, and Coaching

Fill up with Appreciation

Heat with Passion

Bring it all together with Unity

Create a Culture of Greatness

If you are interested in leadership, sales, and team-building keynotes or workshops based on the principles in *Soup*, contact The Jon Gordon Companies, Inc.:

Phone: (904) 285-6842
E-mail: info@jongordon.com
Online: www.JonGordon.com
830-13 A1A N.
Suite 111
Ponte Vedra Beach, FL 32082

Follow him on Twitter at @JonGordon11.

Sign up for Jon Gordon's weekly e-newsletter at:

www.JonGordon.com

To purchase bulk copies of *Soup* at a discount for large groups or your organization, please contact your favorite bookseller or Wiley Special sales at:

specialsales@wiley.com or (800) 762-2974.

Other Books by Jon Gordon

The Energy Bus
A man whose life and career are in shambles learns from a unique bus driver and set of passengers how to overcome adversity. Enjoy an enlightening ride of positive energy that is improving the way leaders lead, employees work, and teams function.
www.TheEnergyBus.com

The No Complaining Rule
Follow a VP of Human Resources who must save herself and her company from ruin, and discover proven principles and an actionable plan to win the battle against individual and organizational negativity.
www.NoComplainingRule.com

Training Camp
This inspirational story about a small guy with a big heart, and a special coach who guides him on a quest for excellence, reveals the eleven winning habits that separate the best individuals and teams from the rest.
www.TrainingCamp11.com

The Shark and the Goldfish
Delightfully illustrated, this quick read is packed with tips and strategies on how to respond to challenges beyond your control in order to thrive during waves of change.
www.SharkandGoldfish.com

The Seed
Go on a quest for the meaning and passion behind work with Josh, an up-and-comer at his company who is disenchanted with his job. Through Josh's cross-country journey, you'll find surprising new sources of wisdom and inspiration in your own business and life.
www.Seed11.com

One Word
One Word is a simple concept that delivers powerful life change! This quick read will inspire you to simplify your life and work by focusing on just one word for this year. *One Word* creates clarity, power, passion, and life-change. When you find your word, live it, and share it, your life will become more rewarding and exciting than ever.
www.getoneword.com

The Positive Dog
We all have two dogs inside of us. One dog is positive, happy, optimistic, and hopeful. The other dog is negative, mad, pessimistic, and fearful. These two dogs often fight inside us, but guess who wins? The one you feed the most. *The Positive Dog* is an inspiring story that not only reveals the strategies and benefits of being positive, but also an essential truth: being positive doesn't just make you better; it makes everyone around you better.
www.feedthepositivedog.com

The Carpenter
The Carpenter is Jon Gordon's most inspiring book yet—filled with powerful lessons and success strategies. Michael wakes up in the hospital with a bandage on his head and fear in his heart after collapsing during a morning jog. When Michael finds out the man who saved his life is a carpenter, he visits him and quickly learns that he is more than just a carpenter; he is also a builder of lives, careers, people, and teams. In this journey, you will learn timeless principles to help you stand out, excel, and make an impact on people and the world.
www.carpenter11.com

The Hard Hat
A true story about Cornell lacrosse player George Boiardi, *The Hard Hat* is an unforgettable book about a selfless, loyal, joyful, hard-working, competitive, and compassionate leader and teammate, the impact he had on his team and program, and the lessons we can learn from him. This inspirational story will teach you how to build a great team and be the best teammate you can be.
www.hardhat21.com

You Win in the Locker Room First
Based on the extraordinary experiences of NFL Coach Mike Smith and leadership expert Jon Gordon, *You Win in the Locker Room First* offers a rare, behind-the-scenes look at one of the most pressure-packed leadership jobs on the planet, and what leaders can learn from these experiences in order to build their own winning teams.
www.wininthelockerroom.com

Life Word
Life Word reveals a simple, powerful tool to help you identify the word that will inspire you to live your best life while leaving your greatest legacy. In the process, you'll discover your *why*, which will help show you how to live with a renewed sense of power, purpose, and passion.
www.getoneword.com/lifeword

The Power of Positive Leadership
The Power of Positive Leadership is your personal coach for becoming the leader your people deserve. Jon Gordon gathers insights from his bestselling fables to bring you the definitive guide to positive leadership. Difficult times call for leaders who are up for the challenge. Results are the byproduct of your culture, teamwork, vision, talent, innovation, execution, and commitment. This book shows you how to bring it all together to become a powerfully positive leader.
www.powerofpositiveleadership.com

The Energy Bus Field Guide
The Energy Bus Field Guide is your roadmap to fueling your life, work, and team with positive energy. The international bestseller, *The Energy Bus*, has helped millions of people from around the world shift to a more positive outlook. This guide is a practical companion to help you *live and share* the ten principles from *The Energy Bus* every day, with real, actionable steps you can immediately put into practice in your life, work, team, and organization.

The Power of a Positive Team
In *The Power of a Positive Team*, Jon Gordon draws upon his unique team building experience, as well as conversations with some of the greatest teams in history, to provide an essential framework of proven practices to empower teams to work together more effectively and achieve superior results.
www.PowerOfAPositiveTeam.com

The Coffee Bean
From bestselling author Jon Gordon and rising star Damon West comes *The Coffee Bean:* an illustrated fable that teaches readers how to transform their environment, overcome challenges, and create positive change.

The Energy Bus for Kids
The illustrated children's adaptation of the bestselling book, *The Energy Bus*, tells the story of George, who, with the help of his school bus driver, Joy, learns that if he believes in himself, he'll find the strength to overcome any challenge. His journey teaches kids how to overcome negativity, bullies, and everyday challenges to be their best.
www.EnergyBusKids.com

Thank You and Good Night
Thank You and Good Night is a beautifully illustrated book that shares the heart of gratitude. Jon Gordon takes a little boy and girl on a fun-filled journey from one perfect moonlit night to the next. During their adventurous days and nights, the children explore the people, places, and things they are thankful for.

The Hard Hat for Kids
The Hard Hat for Kids is an illustrated guide to teamwork. Adapted from the bestseller *The Hard Hat*, this uplifting story presents practical insights and life-changing lessons that are immediately applicable to everyday situations, giving kids—and adults—a new outlook on cooperation, friendship, and the selfless nature of true teamwork.
www.HardHatforKids.com